THE
PUBLIC
LIBRARY
START-UP
GUIDE

Christine Lind Hage

American Library Association
Chicago 2004

Christine Lind Hage is the director of the Clinton-Macomb Public Library in Clinton Township, Michigan, and has worked in libraries for more than thirty-two years. She has extensive experience in creating new libraries and library facilities. A past president of the Public Library Association and an American Library Association Councilor, she also has been active in state, regional, and national library associations. She is the author of several articles on public libraries and is a frequent speaker at library conferences and a contributor to PUBLIB.

While extensive effort has gone into ensuring the reliability of information appearing in this book, the publisher makes no warranty, express or implied, on the accuracy or reliability of the information, and does not assume and hereby disclaims any liability to any person for any loss or damage caused by errors or omissions in this publication.

Composition and design by ALA Editions in Helvetica and Bembo using QuarkXPress 5.0 for the PC

Printed on 50-pound white offset, a pH-neutral stock, and bound in 10-point coated cover stock by Victor Graphics

The paper used in this publication meets the minimum requirements of American National Standard for Information Sciences—Permanence of Paper for Printed Library Materials, ANSI Z39.48-1992. ∞

Library of Congress Cataloging-in-Publication Data

Hage, Christine Lind.
    The public library start-up guide / Christine Lind Hage.
      p. cm.
    Includes index.
    ISBN 0-8389-0866-7
    1. Public libraries--Administration—Handbooks, manuals, etc.
    2. Public libraries—United States—Administration—Handbooks, manuals,
    etc. I. Title.
    Z678.H34 2003
    025.1'974—dc22   2003015462

Printed in the United States of America

08 07 06 05 04   5 4 3 2 1

This book is dedicated to my parents
Letizia Lydia Lind for taking me
to the public library as a child,

AND

Richards I. Lind for his firm commitment
to funding all of my education.

Contents

Preface

Library practitioners, civic organizations, and community leaders regularly contact the American Library Association (ALA) looking for an "instruction manual" to begin or expand a library. *The Public Library Start-Up Guide* serves the ongoing need for step-by-step guidance on starting libraries literally from the ground up.

As a recent past president of the Public Library Association with over thirty-two years of public library experience including a start-up, I have learned important lessons in public relations, librarianship, and "hard hat construction" issues as they pertain to library building, collection development, and community support projects. When ALA first approached me about writing this book, I was immersed in starting a library system in a community that was rapidly outgrowing its existing library facility and collection. I deferred writing the book for about a year. No sooner had I agreed to it than I found myself thrust into a massive building project for two new branches and a new main library. The truth is that I'd rather direct a project than labor at the word processor. So the building project was not only a practical testing ground for my ideas, but also a delightful distraction from the keyboard.

When I use the phrase *library building,* I refer not only to constructing or expanding facilities and collections, but also to building an effective and informed network of professionals, volunteers, and policy makers who are equipped to wisely guide library projects. The ideas expressed in this book can serve as discussion points on starting a library. They are not meant to be prescriptive because libraries must reflect the communities they serve. Some decisions about the direction of a building project are made based on community research, others on the lessons learned by professionals who have worked on a number of projects, and still others—out of necessity—will be made based on intuition. There is no one perfect model for a public library, but there is one truism: Each community deserves a great library that specifically meets the needs of that community.

Experienced librarians will benefit from this book because starting from the ground up brings a new set of challenges, distinct from those of managing an existing library. I have also written the book for the friends of libraries, library board members, policy makers, and governing authorities who want to create and better understand quality library systems. Just as the first American public library was started by energetic and visionary laypeople, public libraries continue to be spawned by the energy and dedication of local laypeople who understand the value and benefits that libraries bring to a community. I hope to help these people consider the different ways to organize, finance, staff, or create a public library to meet the needs of customers and the community.

Since deciding in the second grade to be a librarian, I have worked my way through every level of library patronage and service and gained a wide perspective on what libraries mean to individuals, communities, and the greater society. I have been fortunate to work in four rapidly growing communities with strong interests in improving library services, resources, and facilities. These opportunities have allowed me to guide the construction and collection development of four new library facilities ranging in size from 7,400 to 84,000 square feet. I have worked with staff and governing boards that are entrenched in tradition and habit, and I have also directed programs to build a library system literally from the ground up, including hiring new staff, writing new policies and procedures, and directing collection development for communities that were yet to define themselves. I have served in communities with varied economic circumstances and ethnic diversity and have been fortunate that the majority of communities have allocated appropriate financial resources to library service. I have also discovered that one can learn as much from communities that are apathetic about their library system as one can from communities that are enthusiastic in their appreciation and support of great libraries. I have enjoyed helping to provide communities with great libraries and have learned from those that did not.

I am sincerely dedicated to public librarianship and hope this book will convey my love of and commitment to providing enriched and informed public library service for everyone. Starting a public library is a challenge, but the rewards are innumerable in terms of the joy libraries bring to readers, the information they provide to a free society, and the foundation they build for knowledge and information sharing. Libraries—even the most humble—are the foundation of a literate citizenry and therefore of a free and informed society.

I wish to acknowledge the help of Charlaine Ezell and Caroline Lind Stern who read several rough drafts of this book and offered friendly support, comments, corrections, and suggestions. I am also grateful to my friend and colleague Larry Neal for technological support in all phases of my computing life.

1

Public Libraries:
The People's Library

There certainly is no single right way to create a public library. There are certain elements that are common in all public libraries, but as American history has shown, good public libraries cannot be made with cookie cutters to all come out the same. Each library collects materials, organizes those materials, and makes those materials available to people in a specific geographic area. Another characteristic of American public libraries is that they are supported through public funding. This is not to say that public funding is the sole source of funding, but it does remain the major source of revenue for most public libraries. Beyond these common points, each library should be and is unique.

The public library is an institution created for the people and by the people of a specific community. A community's uniqueness and influence are reflected not only in the physical appearance of its public buildings, including its public library, but also in the types of materials the library collects, the manner in which those materials are organized, and the way in which library services are delivered. The services and resources needed in a sophisticated, multicultural, multilingual urban library differ greatly from those offered in a small, rural community. The approach to service also will be different. The staff of the small library is often able to provide highly personalized service to its customers, whereas the larger library's staff may serve thousands of library customers daily.

THE ORIGIN OF PUBLIC LIBRARIES IN AMERICA

Public libraries as we know them today are deeply rooted in the history of the United States and reflect the people and communities they serve. From the time of the earliest English settlers, there was an interest in the collecting and sharing of books. These settlers brought small personal libraries to North America, some of which became the foundation for some of the great universities of the world. "The first library in America was founded in 1638 at Harvard University. A few churches also established small parish libraries in the colonial period, but these had little effect on the average man."[1]

A quasi-public library existed in "church or parish libraries, which were instituted early in the eighteenth century in the South, particularly in North Carolina and Maryland, by Dr. Thomas Bray, secretary of the British Society for the Propagation of the Gospel. Many of these book collections were itinerant or traveling libraries and predated the social and town libraries of New England by a century or more. However, they proved to be a sporadic effort and gradually disappeared to be replaced by more popular forms of library service."[2]

TOWN LIBRARIES

Town libraries, essentially consisting of gift books, were started in the early eighteenth century in Boston, Concord, and Oxford, Massachusetts, and in New Haven, Connecticut. These generally small collections were not developed with an intention to serve the public, but usually were bequeathed to a town upon the death of a wealthy citizen.[3]

"Prior to the 1850s the phrase 'public library' meant a library that was a private library available to a few but not to all; after 1850 it came to mean a library financially supported by taxation whose book collection was available free of charge."[4] Although available to the general population, these libraries are not considered true public libraries because they did not receive regular public funding. The collections reflected the interests of the individual donor and were not tailored to the specific needs or interests of the community as a whole. Furthermore, these town libraries tended to focus on the circulation of already-owned materials and did not reflect a purposeful plan for development of the collection. Printed materials were limited in colonial America, so the town libraries tended to rely on donations.

Ben Franklin's subscription library is the best-known example of a social library. "Finding that books were expensive and hard to get hold of in colonial Philadelphia, Franklin hit on the idea of pooling the resources of a number of young men, who banded together in 1731 to start a subscription library, the Philadelphia Library Company. The pattern established by that group was followed again and again. These social libraries were not public libraries but rather their forerunners."[5]

Rooted as these first social libraries were in the voluntary association of individuals for discussion and mutual enlightenment, they strove toward two objectives. First, they attempted to satisfy a need of the colonists for group activity. Second, they sought to meet the demand for books, which were at best not too plentiful.[6] The social libraries contained books of interest to the library's specific membership. The collections may have focused on theology, politics, history, science, or even literature, but not necessarily all of these subjects. Collection development depended on the interests of the library's members and the titles available for purchase.

Some social libraries evolved into public libraries. On April 9, 1810, the citizens of Salisbury, Connecticut, voted to spend $100 to buy books for the Bingham Library for Youth.[7] A youth library was also established with public funds in Lexington, Massachusetts, in 1827. Even though the Salisbury and Lexington libraries received public money, they were not established as public libraries, because they did not receive regular, ongoing support from the local government.

THE FIRST TAX-SUPPORTED PUBLIC LIBRARY

In 1833, the 1,984 residents of Peterborough, New Hampshire, recognizing the need for public information in the form of books that would be available to everyone at no charge, approved the first tax to support a free public library. An appointed library board governed the Peterborough Town Library. These two features—*regular tax support* and a *governing library board*—created the foundation for today's American public library.

THE GROWTH OF THE PUBLIC LIBRARY

The nineteenth century saw the rise of compulsory elementary public education, for both men and women. By 1850, when the U.S. census first recorded figures on literacy, over 87 percent of all white women in America aged twenty years could read and write. There was only a marginal difference in the literacy rate between men and women.[8] Institutions of higher education opened for women (Mount Holyoke Female Seminary, 1837; Vassar, 1861; Wellesley, 1870; Smith, 1871; and Bryn Mawr, 1885).

The availability of a variety of educational opportunities had other consequences in addition to higher literacy rates. "The very fact that literally thousands of women in the course of the 1870s and 1880s were brought together in colleges and universities laid the ground for a fresh outlook among women. For one thing, the college experience set them apart from other women of their age and from their mothers and previous generations of women. Many of them wanted to continue this new relationship somehow, and also to put to social and individual use their newly acquired skills and awareness."[9]

"Women's clubs began inconspicuously enough in the 1860s, and without any long-range purpose behind them. But by the 1890s they had become a force of significance in many communities, where the club women became active in all kinds of civic improvement and municipal reform."[10]

In the 1880s, America moved from an agrarian society to a more industrialized, urban society. Families were smaller. Housekeeping was easier and took less time with the introduction of the lockstitch sewing machine (1832), the washing machine (1858), the carpet sweeper (1876), and gas lighting and the decline of manual candle making. A second wave of household conveniences evolved with the distribution of electricity in New York City from Thomas A. Edison's power plant (1882) and with William S. Hadaway Jr.'s electric stove (1896). These household appliances made women's lives easier and created free time, so more women took advantage of the educational opportunities that were available. Women also began to engage in educational, social, and civic activities.

In the 1870s, when educated women advocated their establishment, lyceums and literary societies became popular and were seen as a form of continuing education for both men and women. Garden clubs and book discussion clubs became more educational in focus and turned to more civic-minded purposes. Debates, discussions, panel presentations, and book talks also became popular in the mid-nineteenth century. The literary societies became a source of education for women as well as a social activity. "In 1890 an organization known as the General Federation of Women's Clubs reflected the existence of clubs in great enough numbers to warrant federation. ... By 1910, over one million American women had become club members."[11] Many women's organizations became catalysts for change within their communities. Whether serving the poor, the young, or the immigrant, or being devoted to social change in the areas of the abolition of slavery, women's suffrage, public health, or public education, the women's organizations became a positive force in society.

By the turn of the twentieth century, Americans were beginning to focus less on the establishment of new towns and more on the civic improvement of existing towns. In addition to encouraging self-improvement and continuing education, the members of literary societies and women's clubs were interested in civic improvement. In many communities it was because of the efforts of socially conscious women and women's organizations that the need for a public library was recognized and that the dream of a public library became a reality. Serious fund-raising and many hours of volunteer work created public libraries in many communities.

Not all libraries were started through group efforts. The most notable contributor in this area was certainly Andrew Carnegie, whose philanthropic efforts in the late 1800s and early 1900s helped build 2,811 libraries.[12] Carnegie's library philanthropy was informed by general trends in late-nineteenth-century American culture, particularly a widespread concern for making library facilities available to the public free of charge.

Touched by the mania for efficiency that characterized the early twentieth century, Carnegie used the metaphor of the corporation to reform the practices of American philanthropy. In the process he redirected the course of American library design and redefined the nature of library use.[13] In the twentieth century, Carnegie changed his library design, making it more welcoming and less corporate in appearance. Gone were the high domes, classical porticoes, and monumental stairs that graced the earlier buildings. The plans suggested for Carnegie libraries included meeting room space, open book stacks, and a central desk on the first floor, which allowed easy supervision.[14] This plan also supported the trend toward creating a facility to bring people and books together, rather than to protect books from the general public. No longer were books chained to reading stands or shelved in locked rooms. Books were now out on open shelves in large reading rooms and easily available for public use.

Carnegie provided the construction money for library facilities, while the community provided the property and stocked the library with books and furnishings. The community had to pledge annual funding to operate the library, and community leaders had to commit their time and talent to the operation of the library. This community involvement was embodied in the formation of a library board of trustees, a form of library governance unique to American public libraries.

In 1938, Dr. Alvin Johnson, then director of the New School for Social Research in New York City, published *The Public Library: A People's University* (American Association for Adult Education). The book described the potential of the public library as a critical component of public education. The title of the book underscores Johnson's belief in the educational role of the public library, supplementing its former role as a place for popular reading. As a result, although recreational reading materials were still an important part of library service, educational and nonfiction resources grew tremendously. Citizens and immigrants flocked to their public libraries to attend classes and borrow materials that would prepare them for the information age.

In addition to the construction of new library buildings around the country, libraries expanded service using book wagons. In 1905, these precursors of today's bookmobile were pulled by horses and traveled rural roads of Washington County (Md.) on regular weekly schedules. In 1915, the Hibbing (Minn.) Public Library introduced the first motorized library bus. Bookmobile service has come into and gone out of favor over the years and, by the end of the twentieth century, it was evolving from merely a book delivery system to a mobile programming and computing space. Rural libraries were not the only providers of bookmobile service. Urban libraries used bookmobiles to provide service to special populations, such as day-care and senior citizen centers. In some cases, bookmobiles have been parked in one location to provide temporary branch service while a permanent library is under construction.

In the mid-1970s, Fred Goodman created the street corner kiosk library. This 160-square-foot structure featured glass walls and rotating book carousels that could accommodate collections of about 5,000 items. The library could be operated by a single staff member. Kiosk libraries were opened in Washington, D.C., Georgia, and Florida. The intimate setting provided one-on-one library service in highly trafficked areas, such as subway stations and shopping centers. In essence these kiosk libraries became bookmobiles without wheels. Later, the kiosk libraries, under the name Porta-Structures, evolved into pre-engineered buildings that covered 296 square feet and held 11,000 books. Some communities were able to achieve 125,000 circulations from the small structures. Eventually, the small libraries began to compete with bookstores and grew to over 4,000 square feet.

Today, many library systems are opening small, popular-materials centers and clustering these branches around regional libraries. Larger library systems, like those of Hennepin County (Minn.) and Chicago, have found this is a way to reach deep into neighborhoods and provide reference materials as well as popular materials.

In 1993, the Computers in Libraries conference in Washington, D.C., highlighted the "virtual library" concept. Seeing a way to offer reference materials via the Internet, librarians began to develop Internet sites based on gopher software. By 1995, many libraries were using the World Wide Web as a rich source of reference materials. Net-savvy librarians found that as many as 50 percent of reference questions could be answered using electronic resources rather than print books. Print reference collections began to shrink, and electronic resources took on greater importance in reference service.

In 1997, Fred Goodman's public information kiosk, now known as the "e-branch library," made its appearance in malls, government centers, and public spaces. These small, freestanding units featured CD-ROMs and Internet technology and allowed library customers to search remote databases and then print out information. Credit and debit card hardware allowed libraries a cost recovery mechanism for printing.

The 1990s brought a tremendous amount of library construction. Many larger urban libraries built new headquarter libraries. Many suburban communities expanded facilities built in the 1960s and 1970s. Even with all the advantages offered by the Internet, library buildings continue to grow to accommodate ever-growing print collections and electronic workstations for the public. Fears that the Internet would make public libraries unnecessary have proven wrong.

CONCLUSION

Public libraries continue to flourish in communities all over America. In 1996, there were 9,074 public libraries (administrative entities) in the fifty states and the District of Columbia. There are 16,220 total stationary outlets and 907 bookmobiles.[15] One would think that by this time just about every community in the United States would be served by a public library, but in fact this is not the case. Approximately 13.1 million people in the United States are not served by a local public library.[16] Residents in unserved areas may purchase a library card from a neighboring community or may rely upon their state library, local university, school library, or corporate library for service. But the missions of academic, school, and special libraries differ from those of public libraries and, by necessity, their collections, services, and programs also differ. This leaves many citizens not just unserved, but underserved.

By providing materials, services, and programs, the public library continues to serve all people, without regard to race, religion, or economic status.

Whether formed by our colonial forebears or by groups of interested people today, the public library continues to be one of the primary forces of a democratic society. The public library enhances the general quality of life and property value and can become a focal point of any community.

NOTES

1. Paul Dickson, *The Library in America: A Celebration in Words and Pictures* (New York: Facts on File, 1986), 1.
2. Ernestine Rose, *The Public Library in American Life* (New York: Columbia University Press, 1954), 16.
3. Jesse H. Shera, *Foundations of the Public Library: The Origins of the Public Library Movement in New England 1629–1855* (Chicago: University of Chicago Press, 1949; reprint, Hamden, Conn.: Shoe String, 1974).
4. Frederick G. Kilgour, *The Evolution of the Book* (New York: Oxford University Press, 1998), 130.
5. Dickson, *The Library in America*, xiv.
6. Shera, *Foundations of the Public Library*, 39.
7. Ibid., 159.
8. Carl N. Degler, *At Odds: Women and the Family in America from the Revolution to the Present* (New York: Oxford University Press, 1980), 308.
9. Ibid., 320.
10. Ibid., 325.
11. Ibid., 326.
12. Philanthropy 101: Scientific Philanthropy. 1999. Available at www.pbs.org/wgbh/pages/amex/carnegie/library.html. Accessed 25 July 2000.
13. Ibid.
14. Abigail A. Van Slyck, *Free to All: Carnegie Libraries and American Culture 1890–1920* (Chicago: University of Chicago Press, 1995), 36.
15. U.S. Department of Education, National Center for Education Statistics, *Public Libraries in the United States: FY 1999*, NCES 2002-308, by A. Chute, P. Garner, M. Polcari, and C. J. Ramsey (Washington, D.C.: 2002), Table 2. Available at www.nces.ed.gov/pubsearch/pubsinfo.asp?pubid=2002308. Accessed 17 November 2002.
16. Estimated U.S. population for 1996 less the unduplicated population in recognized public library service areas.

2

Establishing the Library

Today, approximately 13.1 million people in the United States are not served by a local public library.[1] What can communities without a public library do to obtain library service? Individuals and groups interested in starting a public library should first consult with their state library to determine what library establishment laws exist. Every state in the union has a state library (see table 2-1). State libraries are charged with helping establish and improve library service in their state. Laws vary from state to state. The National Center for Education Statistics (NCES) reported that in FY 1999, nearly 55 percent of public libraries were part of a municipal government, almost 11 percent were part of a school district, and 8 percent were separate government units known as library districts. Over 1 percent were combinations of academic and public libraries or school and public libraries. About 6 percent reported their legal basis as "other."[2]

There is no one best way to organize a public library. Some libraries will be better served by having a specific tax levied solely for library purposes. Other libraries might be better off as part of a community's city or township government. In this case, the governing body of the municipal government would be responsible for funding the library. Other libraries may benefit from affiliating with a county library system. Library organizers should be careful to select a model that will provide stable ongoing financial and political support for the new library. Again, the state library can provide direction and assistance here.

TABLE 2-1   State Library Agencies

State	Agency	Address	Web Address
Alabama	Alabama Public Library Service	6030 Monticello Dr. Montgomery, AL 36117-1907	www.apls.state.al.us
Alaska	Alaska State Library	PO Box 110571 Juneau, AK 99811	www.library.state.ak.us
Arizona	Arizona State Library	1700 W. Washington Phoenix, AZ 85007	www.dlapr.lib.az.us
Arkansas	Arkansas State Library	One Capitol Mall Little Rock, AR 72201	www.asl.lib.ar.us
California	California State Library	PO Box 942837 Sacramento, CA 94287	www.library.ca.gov
Colorado	Colorado State Library	201 East Colfax Ave. Denver, CO 80203	www.cde.state.co.us/ index_library.htm
Connecticut	Connecticut State Library	231 Capitol Ave. Hartford, CT 06106	www.cslib.org
Delaware	Delaware Division of Libraries	43 S. DuPont Hwy. Dover, DE 19901-7430	www.lib.de.us
Florida	Division of Library and Information Services	R.A. Gray Bldg. Tallahassee, FL 32399-0250	http://dlis.dos.state.fl.us
Georgia	Georgia Public Library Service	1800 Century Place NE Atlanta, GA 30345	www.gpls.public.lib. ga.us
Hawaii	State Public Library System	465 South King St. Honolulu, HI 96813	www.hcc.hawaii.edu/ hspls/hsplshp.html
Idaho	Idaho State Library	325 W. State St. Boise, ID 83702	www.lili.org/isl
Illinois	Illinois State Library	300 S. Second St. Springfield, IL 62701	www.sos.state.il.us/ library/isl/isl.html
Indiana	Indiana State Library	140 N. Senate Ave. Indianapolis, IN 46204	www.statelib.lib.in.us
Iowa	Iowa State Library	East 12th & Grand Ave. Des Moines, IA 50319	www.silo.lib.ia.us
Kansas	Kansas State Library	300 SW Tenth Ave. Topeka, KS 66612	www.skyways.org/KSL

State	Agency	Address	Web Address
Kentucky	Department for Libraries and Archives	300 Coffee Tree Rd. Frankfort, KY 40602	www.kdla.state.ky.us
Louisiana	State Library of Louisiana	701 North 4th St. Baton Rouge, LA 70802	www.state.lib.la.us
Maine	Maine State Library	230 State St. Augusta, ME 04333	www.state.me.us/msl
Maryland	Division of Library Development and Services, Department of Education	200 W. Baltimore St. Baltimore, MD 21201	www.msde.state.md.us/divisions/lds.html
Massachusetts	State Library of Massachusetts	State House, Rm. 241 Boston, MA 02215	www.state.ma.us/lib
Michigan	Library of Michigan	717 W. Allegan St. Lansing, MI 48909	www.libofmich.lib.mi.us
Minnesota	Minnesota Department of Children, Families and Learning; Division of Information Technology and Library Development Services	1500 Highway 36 West Roseville, MN 55113-4266	http://cfl.state.mn.us
Mississippi	Mississippi Library Commission	1221 Ellis Ave. Jackson, MS 39289	www.mlc.lib.ms.us
Missouri	Missouri State Library	600 W. Main St. Jefferson City, MO 65102	www.sos.state.mo.us/library
Montana	Montana State Library	1515 E. 6th Ave. Helena, MT 59620	www.msl.state.mt.us
Nebraska	Nebraska State Library	1200 N St. Lincoln, NE 68508	www.nlc.state.ne.us

(continued)

TABLE 2-1 (continued)

State	Agency	Address	Web Address
Nevada	Nevada State Library and Archives	716 N. Carson St. Carson City, NV 89701	http://dmla.clan.lib. nv.us/docs/nsla/services
New Hampshire	New Hampshire State Library	20 Park St. Concord, NH 03301	www.state.nh.us/nhsl
New Jersey	New Jersey State Library	185 West State St. Trenton, NJ 08625	www.njstatelib.org
New Mexico	New Mexico State Library	1209 Camino Carlos Rey Santa Fe, NM 87505	www.stlib.state.nm.us
New York	New York State Library	Cultural Education Center Albany, NY 12230	www.nysl.nysed.gov
North Carolina	State Library of North Carolina	109 E. Jones St. Raleigh, NC 27601-1023	http://statelibrary.dcr. state.nc.us
North Dakota	North Dakota State Library	604 E. Blvd. Ave. Bismarck, ND 58505	www.ndsl.lib.state.nd.us
Ohio	State Library of Ohio	274 East First Ave. Columbus, OH 43201	http://winslo.state.oh.us
Oklahoma	Oklahoma Department of Libraries	200 NE 18th St. Oklahoma City, OK 73105	www.odl.state.ok.us
Oregon	Oregon State Library	250 Winter St. NE Salem, OR 97301	www.osl.state.or.us/ home
Pennsylvania	Commonwealth Libraries	PO Box 1601 Harrisburg, PA 17105	www.statelibrary.state. pa.us
Rhode Island	Library of Rhode Island	One Capitol Hill Providence, RI 02908	www.lori.state.ri.us
South Carolina	South Carolina State Library	1500 Senate St. Columbia, SC 29201	www.state.sc.us/scsl
South Dakota	South Dakota State Library	800 Governors Dr. Pierre, SD 57501	www.sdstatelibrary.com
Tennessee	State Library and Archives	403 Seventh Ave. Nashville, TN 37243	www.state.tn.us/sos/ statelib/tslahome.htm
Texas	Texas State Library	1201 Brazos St. Austin, TX 78701	www.tsl.state.tx.us

State	Agency	Address	Web Address
Utah	Utah State Library Division	250 North 1950 West Salt Lake City, UT 84116	www.library.utah.gov
Vermont	Vermont Department of Libraries	109 State St. Montpelier, VT 05609-0601	www.dol.state.vt.us
Virginia	Library of Virginia	800 E. Broad St. Richmond, VA 23219	www.lva.lib.va.us
Washington	Washington State Library	415 15th Ave. SW Olympia, WA 98504	www.statelib.wa.gov
West Virginia	West Virginia Library Commission	1900 Kanawha Blvd. East Charleston, WV 25305	http://library commission.lib.wv.us
Wisconsin	Division for Libraries, Technology and Community Learning	125 S. Webster St. Madison, WI 53707	www.dpi.state.wi.us/ dpi/dlcl/index.html
Wyoming	Wyoming State Library	2301 Capitol Ave. Cheyenne, WY 82002	http://www.wsl.state. wy.us

MERGING EXISTING LIBRARIES

It may not be in a community's best interest to form its own library. In some states, there is more interest in consolidating smaller libraries to form a stronger, slightly larger library administrative unit that can more effectively support local library usage. District libraries that serve more than one municipality (e.g., city/city; city/county; city/township; township/school district) can cut costs by avoiding duplication of administrative and overhead expenses while channeling financial and human resources into direct customer services. For example, in many cases, providing easy access to a single, large, up-to-date reference collection is more effective than providing two smaller collections that duplicate each other. In metropolitan or suburban areas, a community joining forces with another community may be extremely beneficial. This is particularly true when two communities share a downtown, a shopping area, or a school district.

In many metropolitan areas, a large city is surrounded by many smaller municipalities that may form bedroom communities for the urban center. Rather than establishing small libraries that mirror each other in services, the perimeter communities may want to consider consolidating libraries to improve the depth and breadth of service for their customers. Special collections, such as business resources, large periodical collections, foreign-language materials, and low-vision aids, can easily be shared. In addition to saving money by eliminating duplicate administrative structures, the consolidated library may emphasize expensive reference collections, website development, staff development, longer hours, and program planning. Larger libraries command greater discounts on library materials (books, videos, CDs, DVDs, electronic subscriptions, office supplies, etc.). It may even be possible to offer library service from a single outlet for two or more communities, eliminating the high costs related to facilities construction and operation. The small communities of Hartshorne and Haileyville (Okla.) successfully built the H & H Library. This small library has since renamed itself the Hartshorne Library. The Hartshorne Library initially served its customers out of a storefront on Main Street, but in 1998 a new library was constructed that still serves both communities from a single outlet.

The greatest problem in developing a district library through merger is people's attitudes. Library organizers must carefully analyze the benefits, risks, and pitfalls of merging libraries and be able to articulate these to all stakeholders in a new venture. People are often loath to give up their library's independence and autonomy by merging with a neighboring library. Library customers are often familiar with the staff in their local library and may fear losing that contact. A merger may mean closing a library facility—often difficult to accomplish from a political and public relations point of view—and providing access is of paramount importance.

Once the decision to merge two libraries is made, a marketing and public relations plan should be developed so that staff members, customers, government officials, local educators, and media representatives understand fully the reasoning behind the merger.

Growing communities without library service and on the outer rim of a metropolitan area should consider approaching an existing library to discuss extending its service into the new area through a merger. The new community gains immediate access to an established library, and the established library gains a new source of future income.

CONTRACTING FOR LIBRARY SERVICE

A first step toward a single library system for two or more communities might be a contract for service from the established library to the emerging community. In a lightly populated area, the library providing service may be in a business or shopping area used by the emerging communities. Consolidating trips for household errands with visits to the library is very popular. Residents and developers of the emerging community may prefer to go to an established business district for services, while maintaining a more residential environment in the immediate area. Contracting for library service allows both communities to evaluate the relationship before committing to a permanent arrangement.

Contract lengths may be closed- or open-ended. The contract must address access issues (eligibility for library cards, limits to borrowing privileges, access to library-sponsored programs, and fees associated with individual use of the library), input to library governance, costs of the service, and so on. A sample of a very general contract is provided in figure 2-1. Again, local and state laws may preclude this type of contract, but it is definitely worth considering.

FIGURE 2-1   Contract for Library Services

This agreement made and entered into this _____ day of _____, 2004 by and between the _____ and the _____.

WHEREAS, the residents of the _____ are in need of library services; and

WHEREAS, the _____ Library Board is willing to provide full library services to 100 percent of the residents of the _____ in exchange for certain considerations, and

NOW, THEREFORE, THE PARTIES AGREE AS FOLLOWS:

1. Commencing on _____, the _____ Library Board agrees to permit all residents of the _____ the use of the facilities and all other regular services normally provided at the _____ Library, subject to the Library's regular rules and regulations.

2. Upon application and proper identification, residents of _____ shall be issued library cards and shall be entitled to the same rights and privileges, as are residents of _____.

(continued)

FIGURE 2-1   (continued)

3. In consideration of said library services, the _____ shall
    pay the _____ Library Board the following sums
    _____.

4. Said amount shall be payable in _____ equal installments on _____,
    during the term of this contract.

5. This agreement shall become effective on the _____ day of _____, 20___,
    for a term of _____ years and shall be automatically extended, thereafter, for
    ____-year periods. Either party, hereto, may terminate this agreement by giv-
    ing written notice to the other party at least ____months prior to the end of
    each ____-year period.

6. The Library shall provide the _____ with a copy of the
    final financial audit of the Library's operating accounts as soon as possible after
    its independent accountants have certified it after the close of each fiscal year of
    the Library during the term of this contract. The Library shall also furnish, at
    the close of each fiscal year during the term of this contract, its annual report.

7. The _____ shall provide the Library with a copy of its
    budget and its financial statement or audit as soon as possible after the close of
    each of its fiscal years during the term of this contract.

8. This Agreement is the sole agreement between the parties that relates to provi-
    sion of library services. No modification of this Agreement shall be effective
    unless made by an amendment in writing executed by authorized persons on
    behalf of the parties.

IN WITNESS WHEREOF, this contract has been formally approved and executed
on behalf of each of the parties hereto by their duly authorized representatives on the
day above first written.

Governing Board of _____

By _____

By _____

By _____

By _____

OUTSOURCING AND PRIVATIZING LIBRARY SERVICE

A newer, less common, and quite controversial contract strategy is to outsource or privatize the library. The 1997 ALA Outsourcing Task Force defined *outsourcing* as the contracting to external companies or organizations of functions that would otherwise be performed by library employees. In a report to the ALA Executive Board (January 2001), Liz Bishoff and Sally Reed defined *privatization* as the shifting of policy making and the management of library services from the public to the private sector.

Over the years, libraries have outsourced many activities. It is quite common for public libraries to use library jobbers (Baker & Taylor, Brodart, Ingram Library Services, etc.) to purchase books and audiovisual materials. Many libraries outsource their cataloging to companies like OCLC or the Library Corporation. Libraries have contracted for such services as lawn maintenance, snow removal, and cleaning.

Outsourcing has occurred to a much greater extent in a few communities where local officials have contracted with a for-profit company to provide library management and staff. In Riverside, California, the county government contracted with Library Systems & Services, Inc. (LSSI) for library services. LSSI hired the library director and staff and provides services based on locally approved policies and budget. When Jersey City, New Jersey, approached LSSI for management service, a great deal more controversy arose both locally and within the American Library Association (ALA). The local controversy was over the lack of public discussion at the meeting at which LSSI was chosen as the vendor. Within ALA, the controversy has focused on the appropriateness of outsourcing library management.

Whether contracting for management service as Jersey City did, or full library service as Riverside did, careful attention must be paid to the details of the contract.

> Exactly what input will local officials have regarding library policy? A fully privatized library will provide no input from local officials, while a contract for management service may follow policy set by local officials.
>
> What reporting structures will be implemented? Will the library report back to local officials or become a totally independent operation?
>
> Who will respond to specific customer concerns regarding service and long-range plans?
>
> What input will the general public have regarding library operations?

Will the policies, collections, services, and programs offered be designed for the specific community or will a preordained, generic public library be provided?

Outsourcing of library management can have mixed results. In some cases, a community with a poorly run library could benefit from this shift to better management even if it is provided through a management firm. The management firm is a for-profit venture. It must make money to remain viable. A public library with good management is probably going to be more cost-effective.

CONCLUSION

There is no one perfect model for a public library. Each state and community is different, and the perfect library in one town may be completely inappropriate for another town. Library organizers must design a library that best meets the needs of their community. Whether the library is a department of a larger governmental unit and funded from a general fund or whether the library is a separate independent taxing organization will not guarantee success. The true test of a great public library is that it can provide exactly the right service in the right format in the right place and time for the customers who financially support it. If a library meets and anticipates the needs of its users, it is a great public library.

NOTES

1. Estimated U.S. population for 1996 less the unduplicated population in recognized public library service areas.
2. U.S. Department of Education, National Center for Education Statistics, *Public Libraries in the United States: FY 1999*, NCES 2002-308, by Adrienne Chute, P. Garner, M. Polcari, and C. J. Ramsey (Washington, D.C.: 2002), Table 20. Available at www.nces.ed.gov/pubsearch/pubsinfo.asp?pubid=2002308. Accessed 17 November 2002.

3

Building the Team

Gary Hamel says there are three kinds of companies (read "libraries"): companies that try to lead customers where they don't want to go (these are companies that find the idea of being customer-led an insight); companies that listen to customers and then respond to their articulated needs (needs that are probably already being satisfied by more foresighted competitors); and companies that lead customers where they want to go, but don't know it yet (into the future).[1] Companies that create the future do more than satisfy customers; they constantly amaze them.

Our goal is to provide library services that amaze our customers. And we accomplish this through a combined effort. The combination is composed of the board, administrators, staff members, and volunteers. Each group serves a unique purpose. The board is the link between the community and the library. It represents the community in determining library policy. The board members also represent the library in their workplaces and daily lives. The administrators bring professional expertise to the library and formally represent the library in community organizations. The staff members, who may be local residents, implement the policies adopted by the board and provide the daily service. The volunteers are the dedicated people who can truly become our apostles to the community. Successful libraries make use of the special talents of each member or group on the library team by pulling together to accomplish a common goal.

THE LIBRARY BOARD

Board members or trustees serve as the community's voice in library matters, and the board should represent the community demographically. Regardless of whether the library board is appointed or elected, it behooves library administrators and staff members to be involved in the recruitment of quality library board trustees to ensure that they reflect community interests and have specific skills that will help the board perform better. The best trustees

1. Have an interest in the library, in the community, and in the relationship of the library to the community.
2. Are willing to devote time and effort to carrying out the duties of trusteeship.
3. Recognize the importance of the library as a center of information, community culture, recreation, and continuing education.
4. Have a close acquaintance with the local community's social and economic conditions and with groups within the community.
5. Can work well with others, including fellow board members, librarians and staff members, and the public.
6. Have an open mind, intellectual curiosity, and respect for the opinions of others.
7. Have both the initiative and ability to establish policies for successful operation of the library and impartial service to all its patrons.
8. Have the courage to plan creatively, to carry out plans effectively, and to withstand pressures and prejudices.
9. Are devoted to the library, its welfare, and its progress.[2]

TYPES OF BOARDS

Depending on how the library was organized and the applicable state law, a library may or may not have a library board. In some cases, the library director reports to a county executive, city manager, mayor, township supervisor, or school superintendent. In these situations, the ultimate *governing board* may be a county commission, city council, township board, or school board. In other cases, an *advisory board* may be appointed or elected to advise the governing board. It is essential that library boards understand the extent of their responsibilities and authority under state and local law. Advisory boards become library advocates to the governing body.

Governing boards must take the responsibility for making the decisions needed for the library to succeed. The governing board of a public library has four main responsibilities:

1. To secure the tools and resources needed to operate a quality library;
2. To advocate for the library at the local, state, and national levels;
3. To adopt policies (for personnel and public services); and
4. To hire and evaluate the library director.

Governing library boards may be elected or appointed. Elected library boards have greater autonomy than appointed boards as appointed trustees may perceive some obligation to the individual or body that made the appointment. Elected boards answer to the general electorate of the library service area and owe their allegiance to that electorate as a whole rather than to the special interests of an appointing body. Figure 3-1 describes the key characteristics of successful library trustees.

Some cooperative and friendly boards have been replaced by upwardly mobile politicians, persons elected or appointed because of special interests, or those interested in power and whose hidden agendas have more to do with ego gratification than with the welfare of the library.[3] Thankfully this type of board is not the norm. Most library board members recognize their obligation to be stewards for the entire library service area. They understand that the library board supports public library service to everyone in the community and makes decisions that are best for the library and the community as a whole.

FIGURE 3-1 Twelve Golden Rules for Board Members

1. *A trustee must have an interest in the library.* Does she or he believe enough in the educational, informational, and recreational role of the library to fight for the library as the church member fights for her or his church, the school person for her or his educational program, the doctor for her or his patient? It is a duty of the trustee to do so.
2. *A trustee must have time to give to the library.* Continuity of policy is almost impossible if a board member is absent two out of three meetings. No citizen should accept appointment as a library trustee if she or he does not intend to come regularly to meetings. Likewise, a trustee who finds new interests interfering with attendance should resign.
3. *A trustee must consider the position not a matter of prestige but an opportunity for courageous and forward-looking efforts to push the library ahead.* An ideal trustee is a good businessperson, is interested in education, has few prejudices, and has good judgment, sound character, common sense, and public spirit. A trustee should be chosen with these personal qualities in mind and not because of the church she or he attends, the section of town in which she or he lives, her or his political party affiliations, and so on.
4. *A trustee must know the law under which the library is organized.*

(continued)

FIGURE 3-1   (continued)

5. *A trustee serves without compensation.*

6. *A trustee carries a full share of responsibility as a board member, assuring that a few members do not have to do all the work or take all the blame or praise.*

7. *A trustee does not voice her or his opposition or criticism, either publicly or privately, after a policy or rule is adopted by a majority vote of the board.*

8. *A trustee is careful to keep confidential information confidential and does not give out information regarding future board actions or plans.*

9. *A trustee treats the staff members and the librarian in a completely impersonal fashion.* Under no circumstances does a trustee listen to grievances of staff members or treat individual problems on her or his own. The librarian is in charge of the staff and has administrative control until a grievance is presented to the library board as a whole.

10. *A trustee should know the funding sources of the library and be familiar with the library budget.*

11. *A trustee must know the needs of the library and community and be aware of trends and new procedures in the library field.* The best and perhaps only way to do this is to read professional library publications, meet with trustees of other libraries, visit other libraries, and attend the annual conferences and meetings of trustees and librarians.

12. *A trustee knows that all powers are always vested in the library board and none at all in the individual board member.* The individual has no power to act for the library in any way, unless authorized by the board itself; it is always the board as a unit that holds the responsibility and the powers.

TRUSTEES

To help ensure that the entire community is represented, a good board reflects the diversity in the community. It is a good idea to have trustees living in various parts of the community. This will help keep the board informed of issues that may impact only a portion of the service area, but that are important to the development of the library. It is helpful to have trustees of different ages, as this will help the board look at issues from a wider perspective. Diversity on the board will ensure that board decisions reflect community needs and interests.

The mechanics of a library board are not unlike those of other nonprofit boards, school boards, hospital boards, or city councils. Generally the board members are not employed by the organization, but share a common interest in the organization and meet regularly to plan and discuss programs, services, and goals for the organization. They bring expertise from a variety of fields and promote the organization in their personal and business lives.

Many books have been written on how boards should function. The American Library Association (ALA) publishes materials that are specifically designed to assist public library trustees in understanding libraries and the trustee's specific responsibilities. ALA also publishes books listing consultants who work in the areas of library services, planning, and facilities.

Another excellent source of materials on trusteeship is the BoardSource (formerly the National Center for Nonprofit Boards).[4] This organization provides a wealth of information that will help library boards function efficiently. There are many consultants, in and out of the library field, who will work with library boards, helping them organize themselves and assisting with the process of hiring the library director.

Certain housekeeping functions should be put into place early in the life of the library board. The first task is to adopt a set of *bylaws*. The bylaws should specify the authority of the board, titles and responsibilities of the officers, frequency of meetings, date of the annual meeting, rules of order, and the like. *Robert's Rules of Order* has sample bylaws that would provide a framework to build upon. It would be helpful to get copies of bylaws from the state library or area libraries. Officers, typically the president, vice president, treasurer, and secretary, should be elected from among the seated trustees.

Once bylaws have been written, the board should consider establishing some *committees* to facilitate the tremendous amount of work that needs to be done. Some boards work as a committee of the whole while other boards may form ad hoc committees, such as a library director search committee, a building committee, or a fund-raising committee. However, there should be a few standing committees, such as a finance committee, a policy review committee, and a director's evaluation committee. Initially it may be necessary for all committees to meet frequently, but once the library is operating, a committee may meet quarterly or even less frequently depending upon its purpose. For example, the director's evaluation committee and the nominations committee might need to meet only once or twice a year to accomplish their tasks. The finance committee of an established library should meet to review the draft budget prepared by the library director and again near the end of the fiscal year to consider any amendments to the budget. The finance committee also should meet with the auditor before the formal audit presentation to the full board.

In larger boards, committees may want to form *subcommittees*. For instance, the finance committee may form a subcommittee to draft a financial plan and an investment policy if these fall within the purview of the library board rather than a higher governing body (county, city, township, or school district). The policy review committee may want to form a subcommittee to explore benefit packages or specific personnel policies.

Committees should be charged with the responsibility of conducting research, discussing the issues, and drafting proposals for full board consideration. A successful committee structure will allow the library board to accomplish more in less time. The goal is to use the committee structure to keep the board moving forward, not to meet simply for the sake of meeting.

Library supporters should identify individuals who meet the preceding guidelines and those outlined in figure 3-1 and explain the role of a library board trustee and the goals of the library. Based on these conversations, the individual may be willing to run for election to the library board or to submit his or her name for consideration for an appointment to the library board.

Library supporters, as individuals, can help good candidates get elected to the library board, but seated trustees or library staff should be careful to remain separate from the actual campaign. Getting involved in campaign politics can create barriers within the board.

In the case of appointed trustees, library supporters can identify potential trustees and present those names to the appointing individual or body. Appointing bodies often appreciate knowing the people they are considering are interested in the institution and willing to accept appointment. The existing board should suggest appointees who have the skills, demographic representation, and commitment to make the library board most effective.

What skills will be helpful? Individuals with legal, financial, educational, cultural, and real estate backgrounds can help a library board. This is not to suggest that the library forgo hiring an attorney or auditor or other professional consultants; however, it is helpful to have the views of a variety of professionals during board discussions. The best boards are those with a mix of skills and opinions. Through discussion, trustees with contrasting perspectives and viewpoints will contribute to a more informed board and better decision making.

There are certain qualifications that all trustees should have. A good trustee is knowledgeable not just about his or her profession, but also about the library, its policies, and the community in general. It is essential that trustees be very familiar with the library's services and policies so that they can effectively promote the library in the community and make decisions based on current needs and good practice.

Public libraries receive money and land from community foundations, school districts, community organizations, downtown development authorities, and building authorities as well as individuals, which helps start, expand, or enhance the library. This support often comes through the efforts of individuals lobbying the donors on behalf of the library. Library board trustees are perfectly positioned to lobby on behalf of the library without the appearance of being self-serving in a way that library staff cannot.

Library board trustees should have a strong awareness of the politics of the community (governmental, corporate, school district, university). Even if the library is an independent entity, it is important that the library relate to other institutions and governing boards in the service area. Working cooperatively with other planning and governing bodies can bring significant benefits to public libraries.

Partnerships between libraries and other organizations include the use of shared space, joint publicity and promotion, and shared staff and consulting services.

Local municipalities have been known to donate land to public libraries to ensure that the library is placed on a site to the municipality's advantage. The offer of free property should not be the only determining factor in locating a library, but it may enhance a building project.

Finally, a good trustee uses the library. It is not enough that a member of a trustee's family uses the library. Trustees should have firsthand experience with the library's services and collections. If trustees are regular users of the library, they can make decisions regarding library policy more effectively. They can more persuasively lobby government or funding officials on behalf of the library.

Library board trustees can contribute a wide range of skills and viewpoints regarding library matters. They can promote the library to voters and decision makers in a way that staff members and administrators cannot. They can speak to and for the community's residents on all library matters.

HIRING THE LIBRARY DIRECTOR

By using the library and knowing the institution's strengths and weaknesses, trustees are in a better position to hire a library director with the appropriate skills to lead the team of trustees, staff, and volunteers. The library director leads the team and sets the tone for the library's organizational culture. He or she will represent the library to all community organizations. Consequently, hiring the right director for the library is the most important action the library board will make.

The mechanics of hiring a director will differ depending on the library's legal status. County, city, township, and school district public libraries must adhere to the advertising, interviewing, and hiring practices of the parent organization. Relationships with unions or civil service boards will also influence the hiring process.

The independent library may not have the luxury of a formal human resources department, so the board may choose to use a library recruiting company or to handle the search on its own. Whether the library board does the search on its own or uses the services of a professional, certain steps need to be taken before the position is advertised.

The board must first decide what types of qualities and experience it wants the library director to have. Some directors may have personal experience in starting new libraries or managing building projects. Some directors may be better suited to small rural libraries or large urban ones. Some directors will have more experience working in multicultural communities where bilingualism is helpful. The library board needs to determine which qualities and experiences will be most important for its institution.

The board also needs to check state standards for library directors. Some states require that the director have a master's degree in library science and a certain number of years of professional experience. The state requirements may vary depending upon the size of the library's service area or its membership in a library system or cooperative.

The terminal degree for a librarian is the master's degree in library science; however, some graduate schools have dropped the word "library" from their name. In order for trustees to be sure they are getting a properly trained library director, they should contact the American Library Association and request a list of accredited library schools. Association professionals review each school seeking accreditation or renewal of its accreditation to be certain that the curriculum is current and provides the necessary education.

The board's next step is to develop a director's job description outlining the specific skills and experience required. The job description can be used as the basis for the actual job posting. If the board is starting a library from scratch, it is crucial that it hire an experienced librarian. The task of establishing a library or directing a new library can be daunting, and decisions made in the early life of a library will have consequences for years to come. The director will be responsible for drafting personnel and public service policies, putting together benefit packages, establishing an organizational structure, hiring staff, and selecting a technology path for the library. High energy, passion, experience, and vision are necessary for the library director beginning a library. This is not the time to skimp on a salary. Library boards should check with other libraries of comparable size in the state to see what they pay their directors.

So much important work needs to be done early in the life of a library that it is crucial that a board hire the best person possible. The board needs to have confidence in the director's ability to lead the team and to be in agreement with the direction the library is taking. The word *vision* frequently appears in job postings. Gary Hamel and C. K. Prahalad prefer the word *foresight* to vision.[5] They state that *vision* connotes a dream or an apparition, but foresight is more than a single blinding flash of insight. Foresight is based on deep insights into the trends in technology, demographics, regulations, and lifestyles that can be harnessed to rewrite rules and create new competitive space. While understanding the potential implications of such trends requires creativity and imagination, any "vision" that is not based on a solid factual foundation is likely to be fantastical. This is certainly true in the library world. An experienced library director can save a library a lot of time and money by making good decisions through foresight.

Once the posting has been finalized it can be sent to the appropriate advertising sources. In addition to local papers, state job hotlines, and library system newsletters, the board might want to consider broadening the search to a national level. Journals like *American Libraries, Library Journal,* and *LJ Hotline* are the primary sources of public library job postings. It is not uncommon for these journals to have a six-week publishing schedule, so the board must be willing to wait a while for the ad to be widely read by those in the profession. Once the job ad is published, a board should allow at least two weeks for applicants to submit resumes.

Cover letters and resumes should be carefully reviewed to certify that applicants meet the minimum qualifications for the job. Library boards may wish to call on area library directors to assist in the selection process at this time. Area library directors are usually happy to assist in the selection process as they have a vested interest in getting good library directors in their area. People in the field are better able to read between the lines of resumes and may be able to pare the applicant list down to three or four candidates for the board to interview.

On occasion the state library, library system, or other library organizations can offer library boards this type of assistance as well. There also are library consultants who will handle all or any portion of the hiring process for the board. Once the applicant pool has three or four names, the board will want to set up an interview with each of the candidates. The library is an integral part of the community, and as such its director will become a key person in the community's development. The interview panel might be the entire board or a few members of the board. Therefore, the board may want to invite selected community leaders, such as representatives from the local government, school district, chamber of commerce, League of Women Voters, and so on, to sit on the interview panel as well. It is the library's responsibility to pay transportation and housing costs for the actual interview.

Generally the interview will consist of a set of questions asked of all candidates. There are many good books on interviewing that will help the interview panel develop appropriate questions. The best questions should be open-ended and allow the candidate to present his or her philosophy of library service, reveal his or her general management style, and explain his or her fiscal management techniques.

Determining someone's management style is difficult. Some libraries have asked candidates to sort an incoming mailbox and to respond in writing or verbally to each item in the box. Although this is an interesting technique, the logistical and time requirements may pose problems for the interview panel. Some boards have provided a scenario describing a library issue or problem and asked candidates to prepare a sample presentation of a solution to the board, civic leaders, and the press. Candidates are given a computer, printer, easel, markers, and a marker pad to prepare the presentation, which is then actually made to the interview board. Whatever method is used, the interview should be a two-way conversation between the interview panel and the candidate.

The candidates should be given a tour of the library and community, especially if they are expected to relocate to the area. Trustees not involved in the interview panel may want to give these tours. Some interview panels will request a written statement or an oral presentation on some aspect of library service such as the future of the public library. These written or verbal statements can be beneficial not only as an insight to the candidate's library philosophy, but also to his or her writing and public speaking abilities, skills that library directors need to use daily.

Many library associations offer placement offices at conferences. The American Library Association provides a placement service at its annual and midwinter conferences. Applicants submit their resumes at the conference, and interview space is made available to interviewers. This is an easy way to interview candidates from across the country, but does not afford the candidate an opportunity to see a community or the library itself. If a good candidate is found at a library conference, a second on-site interview should be arranged and held before an offer is made to the applicant.

It is essential that the relationship between the library board and its director is healthy, and time spent exploring the potential for the relationship is well spent at this point. For this reason the candidate should be interviewing the board at the same time that the board is interviewing the candidate. The candidate should ask the board members what they would like to see the library doing in the future. It is helpful to know the board's impression of the library's place in the community and the profession. The candidate should try to gauge the board's comfort level with risk-taking and experimentation. The employment relationship is just that, a relationship. Both parties have to be fully involved and satisfied for the relationship to be a long and happy one.

After the interviews, it is time to check the candidate's references. Today's employment practices may only allow former employers to verify employment, but the grapevine in the library world is thick. It does not hurt to ask for references from trusted sources, previous employers, or former employees, even if they are not listed on the candidate's resume. Some library directors change jobs every four to five years in an effort to climb the management ladder. This is not all bad, but it can be a sign that the director faced difficult performance issues. It is better to hire a star who may only be with a library four or five years than it is to hire a mediocre candidate who will be with the library for life. It is essential to thoroughly check references.

Once the decision is made as to the best candidate, it is time to make the offer. A written letter of employment should outline the actual offer. Is the library offering a contract for a set period of time (one, two, three years)? Does the library intend to hire the director on an "at will" or "for cause" basis? What benefits will be available and when? What will the first year's salary be? What is the desirable first date of employment? In return, the candidate should respond in writing accepting or declining the offer.

Once these agreements have been reached, the board can announce who has been hired as the new library director to the community. The hiring of a new library director is a great publicity opportunity for a library. The board may want to call a press conference, which the new director attends. At the very least, the board should issue a press release introducing the new director to the community. There can be newspaper articles introducing the new director and giving background information on both the library and director. Once the new library director is on the job, a second round of publicity can focus attention on the library's bright future. If the board does not have someone who can write this type of press release, ask the new director to write it. Do not miss this opportunity to generate excitement in the community and to have the spotlight on the library.

The library director brings professional library experience and knowledge to the library. He or she will speak for and about the library to the community and the press. He or she will represent the library in local, state, and national library associations. Most important, the library director will select and organize the staff to offer the best library service possible for the community.

Successful libraries create a human connection between library services and customers, and the director will be the key to that connection. The corporate mission has to be expressed from the top down to all employees and volunteers. A commitment to this mission has to come from the board through the director and be communicated to the staff. It has to outlive current leaders, volunteers, and staff.

THE LIBRARY DIRECTOR

Just as the board has specific job duties (assure sufficient funding, adopt policies, hire a director, and serve as an advocate for the library), so does the library director. The director leads the team by setting the overall corporate culture and pace of the library. A conservative, established community may be best served by a quiet and calm library director while a young, fast-paced community may need a high-energy, outgoing library director.

The library director is responsible for administering the resources that the staff will need to get the job done. By developing a financial plan that invests and uses the library's money to the best advantage, the library director can help build a strong financial basis for library operations. By establishing financial procedures, the library director can make sure the library is a prudent steward of the public's money. And by looking for new sources of income (grants, fund-raising opportunities, significant gifts, etc.) or by seeking cost-effective ways to do business (partnering with other libraries or businesses, negotiating discounts with suppliers, or sharing employees or space with other organizations), the library director can stretch the public's dollar to get the most library service possible.

The greatest impact a library director will have on the library is in the type of staff he or she hires. A creative staff offering top-notch customer service can provide great library service, even if the facilities and funding are not ideal.

Just as important as hiring good staff is the director's ability to give staff the latitude to make decisions. The frontline staff interacts daily with the library's customer base. Through their reference work, readers' advisory service, and programming efforts, the staff members know what the customers want. With adequate resources the staff can select and purchase the right materials, plan and present the right kinds of programs, and deliver them in the way best suited to the community. Whether it is home or electronic delivery, in-library or off-site, the staff can match the available resources to community needs, and the library director should provide the decision-making latitude and resources for the staff to perform at its best.

Good library directors keep up with library law, technology, and service developments. Not many attorneys specialize in library law, so it behooves the director to closely monitor legislation at the local, state, and national levels. Most state library associations have committees that monitor library legislation and provide updates to library directors throughout the state. At times, library directors may be asked to write to legislators on behalf of libraries, and all directors should feel comfortable in that task.

The law is not the only area that can change quickly. Emerging technologies, new materials formats, and service developments need to be monitored. The library director with a broader view than frontline staff can track changes in the profession and should explore and introduce appropriate changes to the staff. Often, positioning the library to take advantage of new opportunities is a matter of being well informed and being in the right place at the right time. Through being dedicated to library and professional ethics and being active at the local, state, and regional levels of government and in library professional associations, the library director can position the library to take advantage of appropriate opportunities.

The library director is also responsible for facilitating the work of the library board. In part this is done through collecting and analyzing information, which then is presented to the board for consideration. Library directors may even propose resolutions for board approval. Once the board has approved specific actions, it is the director's responsibility to see that those actions are implemented. The library director usually broadcasts policy changes, board directives, or strategic plans to the staff and to the public.

A good library director brings many intangible benefits to the library, one of which is the ability to create and sustain vitality within the organization. Directors who are energetic and positive about their own work create a corporate culture that encourages staff members to approach their work in an energetic and positive manner. The library director should work with staff and volunteers (trustees and friends) who are having fun and who find personal excitement in creating a vital library.

A good library director makes the right decisions. Those decisions will be based on research, past professional experience, available resources, knowledge of the community's expectations and needs, and ultimately good intuition. Good decisions are not made through good luck, but rather through good thought, planning, and leadership.

A good library director has a passion for good customer service and articulates that passion to the staff. The library director needs to be a role model and set a high standard to ensure that the public receives the most courteous and professional library service possible. From the drafting of policy to the writing of procedures to the implementing of staff training, quality customer service should be the number one priority. It must be woven throughout the organization, and it is the director's responsibility to see that it is.

A good library director works as a team member and supports staff teams. This is why it is important to hire an experienced librarian as the library director. The director should understand the dynamics of the organization and recognize unique skills or attitudes of the staff. Putting together committees or teams to accomplish specific tasks not only gets the work done, but also builds a sense of team within the staff. Cross-departmental committees can be convened to solve problems, plan training, build collections, plan buildings, or brainstorm on any number of library issues. Younger, lower-level employees will approach problems with a different perspective than will older, higher-level employees, but the younger employees' perspectives may be more reflective of the general public's attitude or level of understanding about the library. Frontline staff may have more accurate impressions of customer needs than may a library director who does not work on a public desk. The library director may be involved in some committee work or may delegate responsibility to a staff committee, but it is the director's responsibility to see that committees have the time and resources that allow the library and staff to excel.

A good library director is involved with the community. The staff presents the one-on-one service that takes place in the library, but the library director is the corporate face of the library. By being involved in community service organizations like Rotary, Kiwanis, Lion's, or Optimists clubs, the library director is able to promote the library to other community leaders and to position the library to its best advantage. The goodwill created through the director's community service and involvement may be a deciding factor when the library faces tough issues.

A good library director looks for new ideas from both inside and outside the profession. Library staff focuses on the day-to-day service issues and may not be looking at the bigger picture of society or the information industry. The library director is responsible for seeking out new technology, service patterns, and shifts in paradigms that may have implications for the public library. The director should be involved in professional associations and network with a wide variety of people to ensure that the library explores and takes advantage of new ways of working that will position the organization for even greater success.

A good library director has formal training, experience, stamina, openness, and flexibility, but operates from a basis of passion and foresight. Granted, a library's success will not solely be based on the director, but the director with these qualities will have the best chance of creating a great library for any community.

THE STAFF

The library can have a great building, board, and administration, but if the staff is not outgoing, helpful, well trained, and available, the library cannot succeed. The frontline staff will actually deliver the services to the public, and the manner in which those services are delivered can be a major influence on the library's success. Thoughtful planning on the part of the board and director will be for naught if the staff doesn't deliver the service.

Staff will be responsible for performing the essential work of the library (selecting, classifying, processing, and shelving materials; checking materials in and out; and providing reference service). These tasks must be done quickly and accurately or the library's credibility will suffer. From the lowest-level employee shelving a book in the right spot to the professional librarian providing the right answer in the right format at the right time to the right customer, the library staff is the foundation upon which the library will succeed or fail.

Providing direct service to the public and working with the public on a day-to-day basis can be stressful. Because the library is a public institution, it is open to all people. People with emotional or attitudinal problems are served along with friendly readers who strongly support the library. The library staff member is expected to move from one customer to the next, think on his or her feet, and supervise an area, all while remaining friendly and courteous. It isn't easy, especially at the end of an eight-hour day.

Because staff members are involved with the public most of the day, they become the frontline eyes and ears of the library. They see firsthand how the public reacts to library collections, services, and policies. By passing their impressions of customer reactions on to the library director, staff members can be a key source of information to the library board and director.

Generally, the staff is responsible for incorporating a volunteer corps into the library's work flow. Volunteers must be trained and provided with supplies and a place to work, and their work must be checked. Typically, staff working in the same area will be responsible for this.

Staff will experiment with and have to implement new technology and service models. The migration to a new library automation system will affect all aspects of library service, and the staff will have to identify problem areas and develop appropriate procedures to make sure the library is using the technology to the best advantage. Customer self-checkout of materials or automated check-in and sorting will have dramatic implications for daily work flow and create new service opportunities and challenges at the same time.

Although some libraries outsource their website design, many libraries use their own staff to develop a popular, general-purpose website for the library. Staff will need the technical expertise in human and computer interaction to design web pages that are accessible and usable by the library's customers.

Staff will be responsible for delivering old services in new ways, rather than providing poor service in new and irritating ways. For example, libraries often offer e-mail reference service. Customers e-mail their question to the library and the library provides the answer in a return e-mail. In this newer version of traditional reference service, customers anticipate a response within the same time as if they asked the question in person. The library that only looks at its e-mailbox once a day or less is providing a new service in an irritating manner. Library staff must be diligent about maintaining a high level of quality service, even when working in new areas of technology. The staff needs to look for ways to offer value-added services that are current, relevant, in tune with customer needs, and beneficial from the customer's point of view.

Just as the board is responsible for hiring the director, the director is responsible for hiring the staff. The director needs to establish or review the organizational structure that will best serve the library. The leadership may come from the director, but it is the staff that develops and implements the ideas, programs, and services. It is essential that there is a good balance between support staff and professional staff (degreed librarians as well as people with specialties in technology, bookkeeping, marketing, or the like). Although there is no set formula, it is not uncommon to maintain a rate of two support staff members per professional staff member.

Typically, support staff can be hired from the local community. Public library employees need to be bright people with outgoing personalities, flexibility, and common sense. Working with the public is difficult at the best of times. Library employees need to be able to think on their feet and to treat each customer individually. The field of public librarianship is not for the timid. A bright, outgoing personality is as important as, if not more important than, previous work experience. A reasonably bright person can do almost any job, but it is much more difficult to train a person to smile and to offer consistently good customer service.

The same guidelines will apply to the hiring of the professional staff, although some basic credentials may be required. A library is well advised to invest in librarians with degrees from institutions accredited by the American Library Association. A particular state may require that librarians meet specific certification qualifications. The library may need someone who has specialized training in youth services or has readers' advisory or reference skills.

The library director will hire staff who will do the work of the library. Once again, this is a task that requires careful consideration. Directors and boards should not hesitate to re-post a job if the right candidates are not available on the first initiative.

VOLUNTEERS

Volunteers are the fourth important part of any library team. There is so much work to do in a library that there is always a way to use volunteers. The challenge is to match the volunteer to the right job and then to make sure that the job is of value to the library, not just busywork for the volunteer.

From the library's perspective there are many benefits to having a strong volunteer core. The most obvious one is the additional human power provided by volunteers, but the most important benefit is advocacy. Volunteers can promote library services from the unique perspective of an informed outsider. Friends and family of library volunteers will ask for information on library corporate culture, services, programs, and resources. Satisfied library volunteers can become apostles for the library.

To make the most of these apostles it behooves the library to invest some time and money in making certain volunteers are well informed about the library's mission and goals. It behooves the library to make the volunteers comfortable in the library and help them become members of the library team. Training them well and recognizing their work in public and meaningful ways can easily accomplish this.

Volunteers offer their time for a myriad of reasons. Volunteerism may help them fill in empty hours or provide them with a sense of satisfaction. Forming friendships with people at the library on a coworker basis can expand their social life. Volunteers enjoy the ability to work at their own pace and, for the most part, on their own schedule. In many communities being a library volunteer is a status symbol. Most libraries are successful, attractive community services, and everyone likes to be associated with a successful organization. And for some people volunteering is a reason for getting up and getting dressed each morning.

A formal, written volunteer policy can clarify the library's position on the use and importance of volunteers. Figure 3-2 shows a sample policy. With a volunteer policy in place, both staff and volunteers will have a foundation on which to build a relationship and accomplish appropriate tasks. Volunteers can help in every area of the library. The goal is not to replace staff with volunteers, but to effectively use volunteers to assist staff or to prepare materials for

FIGURE 3-2   Volunteer Policy

1. Volunteers are identified as persons who regularly perform duties or tasks for the Library without wages or benefits other than Workers' Compensation. Community service workers shall work under the same guidelines as other library volunteers. The volunteers described in this policy are different from the Friends of the Library volunteers who are governed by their own policies and bylaws.

2. The Library shall designate a Volunteer Coordinator to oversee the use of volunteers. Each department that uses volunteers shall designate a Volunteer Supervisor to train, supervise, and evaluate volunteers.

3. Volunteers must complete a volunteer application form and be age twelve or older. Volunteers under eighteen years of age must have written permission from a parent or guardian to volunteer for the Library.

4. Volunteers will not be accepted if there is no suitable job match when skills, interests, location, schedule, and transportation are considered. If there is not a job available, the volunteer will be informed that his/her application will be kept on file for one year and he/she will be contacted when there is an opening.

5. Volunteers will not take the place of paid staff and will provide special, unusual, or supplemental services and will be recruited for specific jobs rather than on a general basis.

6. Each volunteer is asked to work an average of two hours a week for at least eight weeks.

7. Volunteers are recognized by the public as representatives of the Library and shall be guided by the same work and behavior code as employees.

8. Volunteers will receive orientation packets and shall wear an identification badge when working for the Library. They shall have access to staff restrooms and lounge during their work hours.

9. Volunteers shall participate in a regular evaluation process and will work under an at-will status and may be discharged with or without cause or notice.

10. At the end of a volunteer's tenure with the Library, the Volunteer Coordinator will conduct an exit interview. A volunteer's personnel file will be retained for two years.

Clinton-Macomb (Mich.) Public Library Personnel Policies, 1999.

---

staff and public use. In the library's technical services area, volunteers can unpack book shipments and assist with the processing of new library materials. In the circulation department, volunteers can check returned materials back into the library, inspect audiovisual materials for damage or missing pieces, sort and shelve returned materials, shelf-read, and assist in checking shelves for items customers claim to have returned. In other public service departments, volunteers can assist in weeding the collection, pulling materials from library shelves for a librarian to review, replacing pages missing from books or magazines, or filing pages in subscription services. In the children's department, volunteers can prepare materials for story time or craft programs, register people and assist in setting up rooms for programs, or help with displays in the library.

Once an individual has expressed interest in volunteering in the library, the library staff should interview the candidate to determine the nature of the volunteer's interest and skills. Some volunteers might be interested in behind-the-scenes work, while others may wish to be more visible and are more willing to work with the public.

Library volunteers should be interviewed just as paid staff members are because a volunteer's previous job skills may dictate the best job assignments. After the interview the volunteer and the library representative may decide that the volunteer's needs and the library's needs do not match and that there is not a place for the prospective volunteer. Just as in any job interview, it is essential that both parties—the volunteer and the library—agree to pursue the volunteer relationship.

Once a job assignment has been made, a thorough orientation should be given to the volunteer. A tour of the building and introductions to the staff should be made, and a mailbox or bulletin board area should be identified so the volunteer will know where to pick up job assignments or general library announcements. Each volunteer should receive a name tag identifying him or her as a volunteer. This name tag may have only the first name on it, but at the very least should identify the wearer as a volunteer.

Job training and periodic evaluation of the volunteer's performance should also be provided. Library staff assigned to work with volunteers should be committed to the use of volunteers and understand the role of the volunteer. Having a specific staff member responsible for this will form the primary link between the library and the volunteer and will color the volunteer's impression of the entire organization.

Regardless of library size, most public libraries have a special volunteer organization called the Friends of the Library. These nonprofit organizations can have a small membership of ten to fifteen people or a membership numbering in the thousands. Friends groups typically do fund-raising on behalf of the library. The most common activity is the Friends' used book sale, but many other fund-raising opportunities exist. Some Friends groups run library stores or cafes and provide programming or publicity for the library in addition to raising money. The best source of information on forming and nurturing Friends organizations is Friends of Libraries U.S.A. (FOLUSA).[6]

Whether involved in the daily operations of the library or in fund-raising tasks, volunteers are an important part of the library organization. Volunteers do not replace paid staff, but supplement the staff. Volunteers are not expected to fund the library, but to assist in fund-raising to underwrite services and programs that might not be available through the library's regular budget. It is hoped volunteers will be so satisfied with their library experience that they will become apostles for the library and maybe even library employees.

CONCLUSION

The goal of a great library is to provide a library service that amazes customers. This is accomplished through a combined effort of the governing board, administration, staff, and volunteers.

The appropriate selection and deployment of the staff is crucial. Sixty to seventy percent of a library's budget is allocated to staff and wages. The governing board's choice of a library director is the key decision, because he or she will be responsible for leading the library toward the right future for that community. The library director will be responsible for hiring and supervising a workforce that will create and offer library service for years to come; a workforce that should do more than satisfy customers; a workforce that will constantly amaze the community by offering top-quality resources and service.

Libraries, like communities, must be dynamic and constantly evolving to meet new challenges and to take advantage of new opportunities and technologies. The library board, director, and staff must be responsive to changes in the community to determine which services best meet the needs of the community. To do that, the members of every part of the team—board, administration, staff, and volunteers—must work together.

Successful libraries connect communities in a way that both shrinks the world and provides access to the ideas that will expand the world. A team that knows where it is going and believes in that direction can convey an excitement and support for the public library to its customers and community.

NOTES

1. Gary Hamel and C. K. Prahalad, *Competing for the Future* (Boston: Harvard Business School Press, 1994), 100.
2. Virginia G. Young, *The Trustee of a Small Public Library* (Chicago: ALA, 1978), 1–2.
3. Paul John Cirino, *The Business of Running a Library* (Jefferson, N.C.: McFarland, 1991), 7.
4. BoardSource—Building Effective Nonprofit Boards [home page of BoardSource], 2002. Available at www.boardsource.org. Accessed 10 November 2002.
5. Hamel and Prahalad, *Competing for the Future,* 76.
6. Friends of Libraries U.S.A., 2002. Available at www.folusa.com. Accessed 10 November 2002.

4

Securing Library Financing

A great library can stimulate economic development, community pride, and educational opportunities and help create a real sense of community. In Rochester, Michigan, for example, the library was prevented from moving out of the small downtown area to a more suburban setting when community leaders said, "Rochester won't be a town without a library!" The library was seen to be so important to the community's viability that the Downtown Development Authority gave $2.5 million to purchase land in the downtown area! Needless to say, the library stayed in the downtown area.

Libraries need stable sources of income. Although libraries seldom say no to a large gift or grant, that type of money cannot be counted on for regular library operations. The dependability of special revenue sources, such as grants, gifts, or fund-raising opportunities, is low. Special funds can support experimental or special services, but steady funding is needed for the essential or core services of the public library. One of the main responsibilities of library administrators and trustees is to secure adequate funding to ensure that their library has the necessary components for success: books and bytes, bodies, and a building.

SOURCES OF LIBRARY INCOME

In FY 1999, the nationwide total per capita operating income for public libraries was $27.20. Of that, $21.14 was from local sources, $3.45 from state sources, $.17 from federal sources, and $2.44 from other sources. As of 1999, Ohio led the country in per capita funding with $55.37. Almost three-quarters of that money came from state government. Mississippi had the lowest level of per capita funding in 1999 with an average of $12.36, and more than 70 percent of that came from local sources.[1]

The Public Library Association (PLA) reports a different perspective on funding. In 1999, PLA surveyed 795 public libraries serving communities with populations between 500 and over 1 million. The average per capita expenditures ranged from a low of $22.03 to a high of $151.98.[2]

These two sources are mentioned because they are easily available and are nationally recognized as the best sources reporting public library statistics, but the information should only be used as a very rough guideline. Great care should be taken in using the numbers from the sources mentioned. The U.S. Department of Education derives its numbers from reports filed by individual public libraries with their state libraries. Data collection is a laborious process, and the information is outdated as soon as it is published. In the 1999 report, some libraries were actually reporting data from 1997. In addition, libraries reporting statistics to PLA were self-selected and represented less than 9 percent of America's public libraries.

Another caveat is to be extremely careful when comparing library budgets. Libraries that are part of a larger municipal unit such as a city or county may receive a significant amount of in-kind service, such as indoor and outdoor custodial and maintenance service, bookkeeping, or human resource services. Independent libraries must provide for these same services from their regular operating budgets. Because these expenses do not always appear in the municipal library's cost figures, the per capita operating expenses from one library may be figured on a base different from that of another library. The amount of money appearing in an individual library budget must be carefully analyzed before comparing it to another library's budget.

The sources of public library funding vary from state to state. In Ohio, over 70 percent of public library funding comes from the state. Arizona and Nevada libraries receive over 95 percent of their revenue from local sources. State statutes usually govern library revenue sources, so it is best to check with the state library to determine what opportunities and restrictions apply in a specific state.

Regardless of the primary source of funding, there are some common sources of supplemental funding:

Friends of the Library organizations often hold book sales and do other fund-raising activities on behalf of the local library. It is not uncom-

mon for libraries to use Friends money for expenses not otherwise
covered in the library's regular budget.

More and more public libraries are establishing foundations or endow-
ments to solicit and manage gift funds. Sometimes this is accomplished through an actual library foundation, but it can also be
arranged through partnerships with other local community foundations. For a small administrative fee, the local or state community
foundation may allow the library to have a named fund within the
larger foundation. The advantage to the library is that the foundation
manages the money in a larger pool of investments and may even
solicit monies on behalf of the library or allocate funds from undes-
ignated gifts to the library's fund account.

Some libraries have been successful in getting grants from various foundations and corporations. Probably the most common grant source is
federal money through the Library Services and Technology Act
(LSTA). This money is available to public libraries as well as school,
academic, or special libraries and museums. The federal money is distributed through the state libraries. In some states, the money is ear-
marked for a single project that benefits the entire state. In other
states, a competitive grant process is used to distribute the money.

Some libraries have purchased real estate and derive monthly rental income from the buildings. Other libraries have become landlords by
renting library space inside the library to for-profit corporations,
such as coffee shops, restaurants, and gift shops, or by leasing space
to nonlibrary-related businesses.

Variety in revenue sources can be very beneficial to a library, for when
one source falters, the others may be able to make up the difference. The key
is to recognize that sources such as grant, gifts, and fund-raisers are supplemental to a steady and stable income source.

How much a specific community needs to run a successful library will
vary depending on the regional cost of living, the size of the library service
area, the population density, and the existing infrastructure of the community.
An old historic building may be more expensive to maintain and operate than
a newly constructed, energy-efficient library. Wages in areas like New York
City or California may be higher than those in rural America because of cost-
of-living issues. Serving customers spread throughout a large geographic area
with difficult interconnectivity (both electronic and physical) can prove chal-

lenging, and libraries in rural America may incur higher interconnectivity costs than those in an urban setting.

A big budget will not guarantee a great library in a community, for money can always be unwisely spent, unwisely invested, or not spent at all. A poorly run library can result, offering services that are not appropriate for or appreciated by its residents or customers. A library with a large collection that is not up-to-date or well organized cannot offer good service. A large staff that is poorly trained or lazy may not offer service as good as that offered by a smaller, service-oriented staff working with a smaller collection. However, a poorly funded library can never be a great library. Limited funds lead to limited staffing. Limited staffing leads to fewer service hours and does not permit sufficient time for quality collection development, customer service, or programming.

Having too much money will never be a problem, but having enough money is a struggle shared by most public libraries. Public library income should come from a multitude of sources that will vary from community to community. Having an annual budget from a township, city, or county, whether through allocation or tax initiative, should be the foundation for library operating funds.

The library director may want to consult accounting books from the library's collection or look at books that specifically address library financial matters. The Library of Michigan has an excellent *Financial Management Reference Guide,* available online, that provides basic accounting information and information specifically pertaining to public libraries.[3]

FINANCIAL PLANNING

Having a stable income source is only the first step to ensuring the library's financial health. The library board should consider establishing a finance committee, which would be responsible for drafting the library's financial plan, managing the library's investments, making recommendations to the full board regarding the selection of an auditor, and making recommendations on the adoption or revision of the library's budget. The finance committee typically meets three to four times a year unless there are special needs (contract negotiations, building campaigns, or regular library millage campaigns) that require the committee to meet more often.

Each library should prepare a financial plan that guides the board and administration in the management of the institution's financial resources. The financial plan should be tied to the library's mission statement and present an accurate picture of existing revenue sources. It should also identify potential future revenue sources. Examples of financial plans can be found in many public and private organizations, and there are books that walk a novice through the process of writing such a plan. These guides outline good financial management principals for libraries as well as provide easy-to-understand explanations of accounting practices and terms.

A financial plan should include a statement regarding the appropriateness of a contingency fund. The need for contingency funds will vary depending on the library's structure, but a well-run library needs sufficient funds to cover major unexpected expenses, upgrades in technology, and other major capital improvements. The library must also recognize that taxpayers provide money for library operations and not to build huge reserve funds. Striking an appropriate balance between savings or contingency funds and ongoing operational expenses is a delicate task. Contingency funds can range from 10 to 50 percent of a library's annual budget, depending upon the independence of the library. If the library is totally independent, a larger contingency should be available to cover unexpected expenses or self-insurance funds. Libraries that are part of a larger governmental unit (township, city, county, or school district) may not be responsible for covering the costs of infrastructure improvements and therefore may not need or even be allowed to accumulate a contingency fund. Some municipal governments require that each unit budget a certain percentage toward the citywide contingency fund. Practice will vary from community to community.

It is prudent to reserve money for major expenses, but the money need not be restricted to those specific uses. Even if the library does not have significant extra money, the finance committee or board should set goals for contingency funds. Libraries typically will appeal to voters to secure funds for major renovations or new construction, but seldom is it realistic to go to voters for money to cover the cost of re-carpeting a building.

Another component of the financial plan is an investment policy. Again, the need for this will vary from community to community. In some situations the library board may have little or no responsibility for the investment of library money. The money may be rolled into city or county investments. In those cases, it would be wise to ask the investing body if the interest earned on the unexpended funds reverts to the library or to the parent body. Some governmental units use the interest to cover the expenses related to managing that money or to cover the cost of doing a library's bookkeeping. Local and state statutes may govern the library's control over the use of interest income.

Tax revenue generally is collected once or twice a year and is spent down throughout the library's fiscal year. It is essential that the library administration, typically the library director or bookkeeper, determine the library's annual cash flow. Once that is determined, the revenue should be in investments that are laddered out to cover anticipated expenses throughout the fiscal year, while at the same time deriving the greatest interest possible. Independent libraries may well be responsible for investing that money while libraries part of a larger organization (city or county government) may not have that responsibility. Law may dictate the types of investment vehicles the library chooses, again depending upon the state where the library is located. State law may even govern the selection of the specific banking institution the library uses. Michigan municipal corporations, including Michigan libraries, for example, may invest money only in banking institutions with Michigan branches. The library's financial plan should clearly state what laws pertain to the library's investment options.

Problems quickly arise when a conservative library board chooses to deposit money with banking institutions covered only by the Federal Deposit Insurance Corporation (FDIC). If a library receives several million dollars of tax revenue, there may not be enough individually insured banks in the state to stay under the $100,000 insured ceiling. Libraries in this situation may want to consider using an investment broker to advise them on ways to broaden their investment options.

AUDITS

Once the library has a secure source of income and a written financial plan, the library director should ensure that an accounting system is set up with appropriate internal controls. Bookkeeping software packages can be purchased for amounts ranging from less than $100 to more than $20,000. Again, one must know if bookkeeping support is available from the parent organization or whether the library works independently from other municipal bodies. If the library is an independent entity, not part of a larger municipal body, the library should contact an accountant about setting up the library's bookkeeping system. There are national standards established by the Governmental Accounting Standards Board (GASB) that apply to organizations like public libraries. Bookkeeping, accounting, and financial management are not covered in depth in typical library science graduate programs, so the library director may have no previous education in this area.

This is also the time to consult with an auditor. The auditor is one of the three people (the attorney and library director being the others) the library board is responsible for hiring. It is the auditor's responsibility to see that the library accounting procedures comply with GASB standards. Library boards should send out a Request for Proposal (RFP)[4] to auditors with experience in nonprofit organizations or to firms that actually specialize in audits for governmental bodies. Check with area libraries, the state library, or the local municipal unit for names of auditing firms, and then issue the RFP. In the RFP, provide general information on the library's financial position, the source of existing funds, the general size of the library's budget, the status of the current accounting procedures, the governance structure of the library, and so on. Ask the auditing firms for the names of their staff who will specifically handle the library account. Once the board receives responses to its RFP, it should schedule interviews with several firms to determine which will best meet its needs and style of operation. As with other interview situations, the board should get references from some of the firms' other clients. One factor to consider when selecting auditors, attorneys, and other consultants is the fee. Fees for auditing services are negotiable and will depend on the scope of the audit required or desired. The fees also may reflect the auditing firm's familiarity with library financial management. If the auditing firm has several library accounts, it will be better able to estimate the amount of time required to complete the audit. That time will be reflected in the fees the firm charges the library for the audit.

This is also a good time to hire a full-charge bookkeeper. Libraries with a small budget may not need a full-time bookkeeper, but it is essential that the library's accounts be properly set up and managed. In fact, two libraries may be able to share one bookkeeper. If the library is newly established, the bookkeeper may be able to accomplish the work on a part-time basis. Larger libraries may be able to manage with a part-time bookkeeper and an assistant who has had some high school course work in bookkeeping and who can handle some of the routine paperwork.

One of the bookkeeper's first tasks is to establish a chart of accounts. The *chart of accounts* is a listing of account numbers used to record the library's revenues and expenditures. This may look vaguely familiar to the librarian, as it is the Dewey Decimal System of accounting. The state may have a standard chart of accounts for governmental bodies, but if the bookkeeper is not able to identify a standard chart of accounts, you should check with your auditor, a neighboring library, the state library, or a local municipality. One library's chart of accounts may be different from any other library's, but it will be much easier to start with a proven chart of accounts that you modify for your particular library situation.

Once account numbers have been established, it is time to investigate book-keeping software. There are several commercially available packages (Quick Books, Peachtree, Fund Balance, etc.). The auditor will be able to recommend various packages that would well serve the library. Check with neighboring libraries to see what is being used. Having a contact person in another library using the same software and performing similar types of transactions can be very helpful.

The library board has the fiduciary responsibility to protect the public's money. The most important element in that protection is to see that proper internal controls are established. Procedures should be established regarding the handling of cash receipts, authorized spending levels for the library direc-tor or other staff members, methods of accounting for daily revenues in addi-tion to the major revenue sources, and the determination of a reporting sys-tem that will allow the board to track library expenditures and investments on a monthly basis. An auditor can help establish procedures to ensure the proper handling of library revenues and the correct recording of library expenditures. It is important that the selection of library materials (books, audiovisual materials, and periodicals), the actual order placement, and even-tually the bookkeeping functions be kept separate to maintain proper inter-nal controls.

The library board should expect to receive monthly reports on the library's financial status. Most of these reports will be generated from the library's accounting software or may be prepared using a typical spreadsheet program. Reports might include a balance sheet detailing the library's assets and liabilities, a year-to-date comparison of the actual revenues and expendi-tures to the approved budget, and a list of the monthly bills. The board's finance committee or treasurer may be charged with reviewing these reports and rec-onciling bank statements to the written reports, but typically the library board at the very least is responsible for adopting the library's annual budget.

BUDGETS

The library director usually drafts the library budget. He or she itemizes anticipated revenues as well as anticipated expenses. Known revenue sources are projected for the coming year, with growth or decreases estimated for each source of revenue. Expenses can be projected based on anticipated staff levels, benefit package premiums, known operating expenses, maintenance contracts, and so on. Again, it is easier to look at a neighboring library's budget if this is the first time the library has prepared its own budget. Programs and services will vary from library to library, but the basics of budgeting will remain the same. The two main expenses will be wages and benefits and library materials; the costs of other items in the budget are much less.

Typically, budget preparation starts about six months before the beginning of the fiscal year. The library director gathers the appropriate information and prepares a preliminary budget. Other staff members, particularly the library's bookkeeper or benefits coordinator, will assist in the preparation. Once a draft budget is prepared, the library's finance committee or full governing board will review and discuss the proposed budget. Does it include all sources of revenue? Are staff wages set at rates competitive in the area, and do they keep pace with the cost of living from year to year? Are there new programs, services, or collections that the library should be developing in the coming year? Have these been included in the budget?

Personnel expenses can be between 60 and 80 percent of a library's budget. Library materials (books, audiovisual items, electronic publications, magazines, and realia, such as puppets, puzzles, and games) may be between 10 and 20 percent. It is common to see about 70 percent of the library's budget allocated to personnel costs, about 20 percent for materials, and the balance for other expenses. But the local library situation contains many variables: the number of buildings and service outlets, the hours of service, the level and adequacy of service, the availability of other library facilities in the area being served, the age and condition of buildings, and others.[5]

Once the board is comfortable with the proposed budget, it is a good idea to hold a public hearing on the budget. In some states this may be required, while in others it may be an option. By holding a public hearing the board offers the library's customers the opportunity to give some input on the future of the library. In most communities these public hearings are poorly attended, if attended at all, but the opportunity for the community to comment on the library budget is a valuable opportunity for library exposure even if few people appear.

Once all the appropriate input has been gathered, the board needs to formally approve the budget and then notify appropriate funding bodies or taxing authorities. The bookkeeper needs to enter the approved budget figures into the accounting software, and staff members need to be notified of their spending allocations. All of this should be in place before the beginning of the new fiscal year.

Budgets are guidelines for incomes and expenditures and can be amended as necessary. Occasionally midyear adjustments are made, but usually the budget is closely reviewed and amended only during the last month of the fiscal year. This type of amendment allows the board to adjust specific line items so that accounts that are overspent can be adjusted with funds from accounts that are underspent. It is at this point that the board may choose to reserve some money for a contingency account.

CONCLUSION

Stable and sufficient funding is essential for library growth and success. Traditional tax revenue sources can and should be supplemented with additional revenue sources such as grants, gifts, and fund-raising, but the library must recognize the instability of those additional sources. Careful financial planning will lead to better long-term security for the library and better accountability to the public it serves. The governing board ultimately has the fiduciary responsibility for library operations, but library administration is responsible for the day-to-day financial procedures. Both the board and administration need to work with the library's auditing firm to ensure that the public's money is properly accounted for and managed.

NOTES

1. U.S. Department of Education, National Center for Education Statistics, *Public Libraries in the United States: FY 1999,* NCES 2002-308, by A. Chute, P. Garner, M. Polcari, and C. J. Ramsey (Washington, D.C.: 2002), Table 12. Available at www.nces.ed.gov/pubsearch/pubsinfo.asp?pubid=2002308. Accessed 17 November 2002.
2. Public Library Association, *Statistical Report 2000: Public Library Data Service* (Chicago: ALA, 2000), 41.
3. Library of Michigan, *Financial Management Reference Guide* (Lansing: Library of Michigan, 2002). Available at www.//libraryofmichigan.org/publications/finmanref.html. Accessed 10 November 2002.
4. Ibid.
5. Joseph Wheeler, *Wheeler and Goldhor's Practical Administration of Public Libraries* (New York: Harper and Row, 1981), 121.

5

Shaping the Organization

"It is the purpose of an organization," writes Peter Drucker, "to make common men to do uncommon things."[1] Certainly the creation of a new library is an uncommon task and putting a great organization together will be the key to a library's success.

What comes first? Personnel policies? Benefit packages? Staff? How does a library attract qualified staff if it doesn't have the first two in place? If the library does not have staff, how does it get benefit pricing and plan options, which are often based on the number and age of staff?

THE LIBRARY DIRECTOR

The process starts with the library director. The director will be responsible for drafting personnel policies, researching benefit packages, writing job descriptions, posting job openings, and hiring staff. If the library is independent, not part of a township, city, or county unit, it probably does not have a benefit package available. To attract a library director, the library may offer additional pay until a benefit package is available. Another option, if the director is coming from another job and is eligible for benefits under the Consolidated Omnibus Budget Reconciliation Act of 1985 (COBRA), is for the library to pay COBRA costs for the new director. COBRA requires employers to offer departing employees, who would otherwise lose benefit protection, the option of continuing to have group health-care plan coverage.

COBRA does not cover life insurance, disability insurance, retirement plans, or benefit time related to sick or vacation time, so the board might want to consider offering an additional amount to cover those benefits.

OTHER STAFF

Once the director is in place, decisions need to be made regarding organizational structure and the hiring of additional staff. Library tasks fall into three broad categories: professional, technical, and support. Professional responsibilities revolve around materials selection and direct customer service in reference and readers' advisory services. Technical positions focus on the management of computer systems and supervision of circulation (check-in and checkout) and acquisitions services. Support staff typically works at check-in and checkout and is responsible for processing and shelving materials. People working in each of these categories will need different skills.

The American Library Association (ALA) publishes *Library and Information Studies Education and Human Resource Utilization: A Statement of Policy,* which recommends categories of library personnel and levels of training and education appropriate for these categories.[2] The statement recognizes the special skills and talents outside the traditional graduate-level library education that are needed by libraries.

Library professionals have a graduate degree in library science from an ALA-accredited program. Graduate programs typically offer courses in the creation, selection, and organization of information and libraries. The graduate-level program is not specialized by type of library (public, academic, special, or school); however, someone interested in public libraries would take the public library courses, while someone interested in academic library work might take more courses in the area of research. People graduating from library school have the same degree essentially, with a few classes that focused on one area of specialization.

The technical staff in a public library may be responsible for bookkeeping, managing computer networks, telecommunications, graphic arts or desktop publishing, or human resources. The smaller library may not have the luxury of having full-time technical staff in the initial stages, but may opt to hire technical people on an hourly basis. Bookkeepers may be hired on an hourly basis and may be able to handle a small library's accounts in ten to fifteen hours a week. Although library accounting is not significantly different from accounting for other nonprofits, it is helpful to have a bookkeeper who is familiar with fund accounting, which is not uncommon in municipal corporations. With the impending changes in accounting rules, library accounting will become more like that for a for-profit organization, and a full-charge bookkeeper should easily be able to handle the library's bookkeeping. In regard to the library's computer systems, librarians, especially those with more recent degrees, may be able to manage the local- or wide-area networks and telecommunications issues. Students with good computer skills may also be willing to manage the library's network on a part-time basis. Also, students with artistic abilities or desktop publishing experience may be able to provide enough graphic arts skills to produce a library newsletter, program flyers, or simple signs. Another option used by some libraries is to share employees with another library or nonprofit organization.

Technical employees needed in a public library might be found in other local businesses or educational organizations, or they may be hired through an employment agency on a temporary basis. Once a library is established and has a budget of $1 million or more, it is recommended that individuals with specific skills in bookkeeping, computers, and graphic arts be hired for those areas in the library. A human resources professional may not actually be hired until a library has more than one hundred employees. Until that time it is not uncommon for the library director to serve as the main personnel professional and for a bookkeeper to function as a payroll and benefits coordinator. When a library has a larger staff or if the library is unionized, a human resource specialist or personnel manager may be appropriate.

Support staff and clerical staff are usually hired from the immediate community. Intelligent and personable people who are familiar with the community make excellent additions to the support staff. Personality, flexibility, and the ability to work with the public and pay attention to technical details are the most important characteristics needed to be a successful member of a library support staff. Some community colleges offer Library Technical Assistant (LTA) degrees. LTAs are excellent candidates for library positions as they have made the effort to train for a career in libraries. Some library cooperatives, systems, or networks also offer training for nonlibrarians, and library directors should consider using those training opportunities for new and current staff.

Staff diversity also strengthens a library's service development and outlook. Public libraries serve customers of all ages, religions, races, and ethnic backgrounds, and the staff should reflect the demographic mix of the community. Younger staff members will be more in touch with the youth of the community, and older workers will share a historical perspective and be more understanding of problems faced by older customers. A mix of religious, racial, and ethnic backgrounds in employees will enrich the services and programs offered by the library. Librarians with diverse educational specialties will enhance the library's collection development. In some communities multilingual skills may be important. Staff diversity becomes easier as the library grows, but even the small library should attempt to provide some diversity.

SCHEDULES

For safety's sake, a library should have a minimum of at least two staff members on duty at all times. With a minimum of four full-time staff members, a library can offer a full schedule of morning, evening, and Saturday service. If a librarian were paired with a nonprofessional staff member as a team, they would start the day and be relieved at lunch with a second team. The first team would relieve the second team for dinner and then the second team would cover the evening. The two teams would alternate Friday and Saturday service. This is not recommended as there is not enough depth in staffing to cover illness or vacation, but it would, in certain situations, work for short periods of time. Libraries that cover the service desk this tightly will find it helpful to establish a list of substitute staff members. Substitutes need to receive training and desk time to maintain that training.

Most libraries rely on a corps of part-time as well as full-time employees. It is not uncommon for part-time library employees to work in more than one library and thus provide the substitute corps for several libraries. It is particularly helpful if the substitutes are somewhat familiar with the library, the library's computer system, and available system, network, or cooperative services. A mix of full- and part-time employees will give the library the maximum scheduling flexibility.

The four-person schedule mentioned earlier does not provide enough off-desk time for staff to do an adequate job of selecting, ordering, and processing materials. This type of work always takes more time than the layperson expects yet is an essential task if the library is to function effectively. Libraries without good collections will have trouble offering good service, and it takes staff time to build a collection. The librarian will select the books, DVDs, CDs, and so on, but support staff can actually place the orders with one of the nationally recognized book vendors. If library staff is limited to four people, the board may want to consider fewer public service hours so that the necessary work can be done.

ORGANIZATIONAL STRUCTURE

Even libraries with few staff members need to have some kind of organizational structure. Typically, small and medium-sized libraries have fairly flat organizational structures. There is no ideal organization structure. The organizational chart should be as simple as possible, and it should clearly and concisely outline the lines of authority. Who is responsible for what, and who works for whom—these are the only reasons for organizational charts to exist.[3]

The divisions of labor determine some libraries' organizational structures. An established library may have separate departments, such as administration, adult services, children's services, circulation services, outreach services, and technical services. The actual organizational structure can vary a great deal from library to library with smaller libraries usually having a much less formal structure. Smaller organizations can function with a higher level of informality because communication is more easily managed among a small group of individuals. The smaller library counts on a higher level of staff flexibility, takes advantage of individual capabilities when making job assignments, and relies less on narrow job descriptions.

However, as the library grows, the organizational structure will change to maintain staff communication, to meet the needs of a new or changing community, to make better use of staff skills, or to work with particular political situations. Each library will develop a structure that works best for the organization at a particular point in time. T. D. Webb has documented the evolution of twenty-two libraries.[4] Sample organizational charts explain the nature of work done in each area of the library and in some cases indicate the number of staff involved in that work. Experienced library directors will be able to develop a structure that they are comfortable with and that will help the library best serve its community.

Many large libraries are organized by subject. Books, periodicals, and audiovisual materials are grouped together in departments, such as business and economics, sociology, science, education/religion and philosophy, literature, fine arts, history and travel, and so on. By using this organizational structure the library can provide specialists in each subject area to work with the public. This is an expensive model to follow because of the duplication of general resources in each department and the need to hire specialists, but when collections exceed five or six hundred thousand items, it helps to break the collection down into smaller sections, and dividing it by subject is one way of managing that larger collection.

Many public libraries rely upon librarians who are generalists. The generalist librarian will have a broad educational background and does research and provides service in a wide range of subjects and for library users of all ages. The small library may have a single information desk where library materials are checked in and where the public can ask for reference and readers' advisory assistance, but as libraries grow it is not uncommon to offer two or more service desks in the building. The staff at the desk closest to the entrance will check materials in and out, issue library cards, manage the phones, and answer directional questions from the public. This employee group might also be responsible for placing orders for new library materials, processing new acquisitions, and repairing damaged materials. Typically, non-librarians staff this desk. Sometimes this department is called support services.

The second desk is typically called the reference desk. Librarians assist customers in locating appropriate information and resources, whether from the library's collection or through interlibrary loan from another library. The reference librarians also are directly involved in selecting library materials for the library's collection.

Initially, staff members will wear more than one hat. A librarian will select materials, answer reference questions, and provide programs of interest to the community. The clerical staff will place orders for the selected materials, process those materials when they arrive, check materials in and out to customers, track overdue materials, answer general phones, and serve as support staff to the librarians. But in some very small libraries, the support staff might also cover the public reference desk. It is not uncommon to hear professional and support staff of small libraries talking about shoveling sidewalks, plunging toilets, and handling programs like story time or guest speaker series. For a new library to flourish, it is essential that the director hire capable people who are self-starters, willing to remain flexible and pick up the slack in all areas of the library as they are needed.

Medium-sized libraries are typically organized by user group. A children's services department will have staff who are trained in storytelling and in working with children. Adult services staff will generally serve students in high school and older. The library may have a special department to serve people with special needs (low vision, hearing impairment, physical limitations, etc.). The department may actually take library services beyond the library walls to shut-ins, individuals who are institutionalized, or people who speak English as their second language.

Libraries are paying more attention to the competition being presented by the mega-bookstores and entertainment centers and are attempting to make the library as attractive as successful retailers make their malls and store outlets. With the increased circulation of CDs, videos, DVDs, and audio books, some libraries have created audiovisual departments that are separated from periodicals and books. Some libraries have created popular materials departments that allow customers to have quick access to popular materials without having to go through the entire building. With the introduction of cafes, library stores, and bookstore-style fixtures and furniture, popular material collections are being pulled together to form a high-traffic, informal mix of library materials.

Depending on the size of the community, library facility, budget, and collection, the library director will determine the best organization structure. The director's next task is to hire the staff to implement the service program. Ideally a library will have two support staff for every professional (librarian with a master's degree in library and information science) staff member. In a well-established library, there might be a higher proportion of support staff to professional staff, but in a library that is just starting, it is better to hire more professional librarians. Librarians can order, process, and check out library materials, but it is difficult for support staff (nonlibrarians) to develop appropriate collections, services, and programs for the community.

Depending on the way the library is organized, the library director may be responsible for all aspects of human resources. If the library is part of a larger governmental body, there may be local regulations that have to be followed. The same would be true for a library that is working in a unionized environment. In some cases, a library's human resources are managed entirely by the parent organization.

JOB DESCRIPTIONS AND POSTINGS

Before job postings are distributed, job descriptions are needed. There are many books that will help the library director prepare the job postings and job descriptions, and many library directors are willing to share job descriptions of their staffs. It is essential that job descriptions and announcements comply with the Americans with Disabilities Act (ADA) requirements, and a fair amount of literature is available on the impact of the ADA on hiring practices. Since labor laws change and hiring an entirely new staff is unusual, it would behoove the library director to brush up on personnel issues. States, counties, library organizations, and chambers of commerce offer continuing education courses on labor laws and personnel management. These same organizations may assist in writing job descriptions or job announcements. In some cases, they may even refer potential employees to the library.

It is helpful if a small list of essay questions is included in the job posting. The purpose of the questions is to evaluate the candidates' ability to follow directions and to write responses, and to discover how familiar they might be with library matters. The responses are helpful in reviewing applications to select candidates for the formal job interview.

Once the job postings are created, they need to be distributed. Depending on the availability of librarians, the library may choose to advertise nationally for the professional positions. There are several national library journals that always include job announcements for library positions. These journals often have six- to eight-week lead times, so the advertising and interview process will be longer than if the job is posted locally. Local newspapers are also a common advertising option used by libraries. It is becoming more common for professional and technical positions to be advertised on library-related electronic discussion boards on the Web and through area library organizations and hotlines as well. Support staff positions are typically advertised in local newspapers or through the library system, network, or cooperative.

INTERVIEWS

The purpose of the interview is for the library representative or interview panel and the candidate to get to know each other well enough to see if a mutually agreeable relationship can be established. Once candidates have been selected, the interviews should be scheduled fairly close to each other so fresh comparisons can be made between candidates. If the job is advertised nationally, the library should be prepared to pay travel expenses for candidates selected for interviews. The interview site may be in the library, in a restaurant, in a neighboring library, or in a municipal building. It is best if the interview is in the library so candidates can actually see the work site. Some library directors prefer to interview potential employees alone, while others may invite a colleague or other staff member to the interview. It is helpful if the direct supervisor is involved in the interview process.

Candidates should show as much care in selecting a potential employer as the library should in hiring a potential employee. Interviews are high-stress experiences for the applicants and can be a high-stress experience for the interviewer as well. The person the library hires today may be with the organization for thirty to forty years. Accurate assessments of a candidate's suitability for the position and organization are crucial.

The resume and job application will provide the factual information on the candidate. The interview provides an opportunity for the interview panel to observe the candidate's communication skills, performance under stress, and general appearance.

It is common for the interview panel to prepare a list of questions that will be asked of all candidates. Open-ended questions allow the candidate to explain past experience and training, communicate his or her philosophy of library service, and express his or her professional goals. The same can be said from the library's point of view. Will the questions identify the style of worker that will best meet the library's need? Some possible questions include:

What are your past work experiences both in and out of libraries? By asking the candidate to provide this information, the interview panel will be able to determine if the candidate has the necessary breadth of experience to perform the job in question. Interview panels that have at least one librarian on the panel will have the added benefit of knowing if the candidate has a realistic understanding of her or his role in previous library organizations.

What do you know about this library? Candidates should make an effort to become familiar with the community and library to ensure that they will be comfortable in the new work setting. It is disappointing for all when, after six months, the library or the candidate decides they aren't a good match, and a little research during the application process might avoid this unpleasant consequence.

What does the public library of the future look like? Here is an opportunity for candidates to state their vision and expertise. If the library is anxious to embrace new technologies, the interview panel will want to see candidates who include those new technologies in their vision of library service.

What do you think public libraries should be doing with or about the Internet? Internet access has brought a great deal of controversy to public libraries. Is the candidate able to clearly state her or his position on access and filtering? Does that opinion match the library's approach to offering Internet service?

What would you do if you heard a colleague give out incorrect information or misstate a library policy? This type of question will test the candidate's commitment to customer service. Will he or she be an advocate for the customer or protective of the staff member's feelings?

If the library administration or board made a decision that was unpopular with the public, how would you handle complaints? What if you also disagreed with the decision? For the library that wants a lot of feedback and input from staff, the answer to this question will provide a glimpse of the candidate's future actions.

If you had to provide reference service from only ten resources, which ten would you choose? Here is an opportunity to test the candidate's familiarity with reference works and his or her comfort level with electronic resources versus print resources. More important than the actual titles mentioned is whether the candidate has a grasp of the range and types of questions he or she is likely to encounter on the job.

When a customer asks you to recommend a good book, how do you respond? This question will provide a sample of the candidate's reference interview techniques whether he or she is working with children or adults in a reference or readers' advisory capacity.

Depending on the type of job being advertised, it may not be appropriate to ask all of the preceding questions, but using a set of questions for all candidates helps determine the candidate's view of public library service and commitment to the profession.

The panel should attempt to determine the candidates' working style. Do they prefer working independently or being closely guided? Will the candidate be able to lead or work as part of a team? Is the candidate a self-starter or follower?

Communication skills, both oral and written, are essential for success in any library position. Whether the employee is the library director or a frontline worker at a customer service desk, the ability to communicate is important. Even with the stress of an interview, it may be possible to judge the candidate's ability to interact with the public. The candidate's comfort level with the interview panel may be an indication of his or her comfort level with the public. Does the candidate make good eye contact with the interview panel? Is the candidate able to listen to the interview questions and follow with reasonable answers? When responding extemporaneously to questions, is the candidate able to respond in coherent sentences? Library employees represent the library at public service desks, at professional meetings, and at various functions within the community, and an employee's ability to speak intelligently and with confidence is a great asset to the library.

By looking at the job application or resume, can assumptions be made about the candidate's writing skills? The library might want to request a writing sample to evaluate the candidate's ability to write. Library employees may be required to write reports for the library board or the administration, press releases for local papers or the library's newsletter, or interoffice memos explaining changes in procedures. The ability to communicate with internal or external customers is an important skill of all library employees.

Working conditions need to be discussed with all candidates. The candidate should be given a copy of the job description that explains what the job entails. What is the expected daily or weekly work schedule? What is the anticipated start date? This is also an opportunity for the interview panel and candidate to discuss the potential role the candidate will have in the library's organization and opportunities for future promotion.

It is important to always check references as not every job separation is voluntary. Request explanations for gaps in employment or numerous job changes. Question jobs that appear to be a step down from the previous job. Interviewers typically call or write to previous employers or coworkers during the reference check period. The interviewer must realize that former employers may be constrained by local policy to merely verifying employment dates. Checking references by telephone often elicits more revealing comments. People are reluctant to put in writing things they may feel comfortable saying over the phone. Also, conducting reference checks over the phone is faster than waiting for traditional mail delivery and responses. A good final question in a reference check would be "Would you rehire this employee?"

ORIENTATION

A good orientation and training program will help the new employee understand the workings of the library and his or her role and its importance to the library. Orientations should be given early and can be done in groups. At the very least, all new employees should receive

> introductions to other library staff members;
>
> tours of the building and general descriptions of departmental functions; and
>
> a printed packet outlining the regulations of their employment, including instruction on recording work time, pay periods, dress code, policies on socializing, expectations for attendance and reporting absences and tardiness, what to do in case of emergencies on the job, and the library's customer service policy.

CONCLUSION

Libraries do not always have great buildings, collections, or budgets, but they must have great employees to be great libraries. This is why the typical library will spend between 60 and 75 percent of its budget on human resources. Spending sufficient time to hire staff with the best mix of personalities, talents, skills, and diversity is essential. Libraries that incorporate this type of diversity within the staff will, as Drucker says, "make common men to do uncommon things" and make great libraries.

NOTES

1. Peter F. Drucker, *The Practice of Management* (New York: HarperCollins, 1993), 144.
2. *Library and Information Studies Education and Human Resource Utilization: A Statement of Policy* (Chicago: ALA, 2002). Available at www.ala.org/hrdr/lepu.pdf. Accessed 17 November 2002.
3. Paul John Cirino, *The Business of Running a Library* (Jefferson, N.C.: McFarland, 1991), 38.
4. T. D. Webb, *Public Library Organization and Structure* (Jefferson, N.C.: McFarland, 1989), 23–89.

6

Taking Care of Business

A public library is like any other business. It needs to have an established line of authority, a good staff, solid funding, and policies and insurance that will protect the employees and the business. Two good ways to protect the business or library are to make sure that the employers and employees know the ground rules for employment and service standards and to have insurance to cover mistakes and accidents that can and will occur.

The adoption of policies is one of the major responsibilities of any governing board. There are two broad categories of policies: personnel policies and service policies. Personnel policies define the relationship between the employer and employee. Service policies define the relationship between the library and the public it serves. Even the smallest library should take the time to develop a written policy manual that collects the individual policies adopted by the governing board so that the administration and staff make consistent decisions. The definitive book on public library policies is *Creating Policies for Results: From Chaos to Clarity,* by Sandra Nelson and June Garcia.[1]

Initially, the policy manual may be fairly small, but as the organization grows, the policy manual will grow as well. Policies may be expanded to detail the library's work environment (union or nonunion), encompass new situations (changes in funding, governance, and labor laws), growth within the organization (multiple layers of supervision, additional locations), or just to respond to questions that arise in the work environment. The larger and older the organization, the more robust the policies become.

Policy writing is a process that begins with research, then involves writing, review, revision, approval, distribution, and, finally, periodic review.[2] There are several good books on library policy development that will help the board and director begin this process. Initially, the library director may draft each policy, but it is essential that policies be fully discussed by the governing board or a subcommittee of the board as well as reviewed by the library's attorney before being adopted by the governing board. A library should have policies in place when employees are hired so that everyone will understand the terms of employment and public service.

PERSONNEL POLICIES

A core of personnel policies should be in place when the library's first employee is hired. Within the personnel manual are two types of policies. The first covers terms of employment and the second type describes the benefits that will be offered to employees. Figure 6-1 lists the items personnel policies will establish.

The type of employment being offered—at-will or for-cause—should be stated separately in the manual and should be woven throughout the policy manual in appropriate policies. In an at-will work environment, either the employee or the library can terminate the employment relationship at any time, with or without cause, with or without notice. In a for-cause environment, the

FIGURE 6-1 Personnel Policies

Type of employment being offered

Number of hours employees are expected to work each week (paid holidays)

Employee conduct while on the job

Summation of employment practices (posting of openings, hiring, transfers, suspensions, termination)

Types of leaves of absence available (sick, vacation, personal business, bereavement, jury duty, military leave)

Terms of insurance policies available to employees (health, dental, vision, life, cafeteria plans)

Disability coverage

Retirement plans

Deferred compensation

employee must give notice (two to four weeks is common) before leaving the job, and the employer cannot terminate an employee without cause. Typically, for-cause statements outline discipline steps as well as severance options and are almost always present in a union environment.

The number of hours full-time employees are expected to work each week should be clearly stated. The range of hours will vary from region to region, but a typical workweek is thirty-five to forty hours a week. This particular policy may also differentiate between hourly and salaried employees. Salaried employees may not work a full week, but may work a minimum number of hours to qualify for prorated benefits. There may be a job category for hourly workers that encompasses pages or shelvers and substitute staff. The policy should state whether hourly employees are eligible for any accrued benefit time (sick, vacation, holiday) or work only on a pay-for-time-worked basis.

Employee conduct while on the job should be explained. The policy may cover such concerns as

excessive absenteeism or tardiness

providing false information on an employment application, time card, or any other record

insubordination

inefficiency, negligence, or nonperformance of assigned duties

rude or inappropriate behavior to or harassment of patrons and other employees

divulgence of confidential information

acts of sabotage or other interference with library operations

removal or possession of library equipment

possession or use of intoxicating beverages, narcotics, or weapons on library property

Library policy should explain employment practices in regard to the posting of new positions, recruitment of new employees, transfer or appointment of employees, and how employee and management disputes will be settled. If the library has rules regarding residency, nepotism, or other local restrictions, they should be included in this portion of the personnel manual.

The types of leaves of absence that will be offered should be detailed in a separate policy. Special mention should be made of the number of sick days offered full-time or salaried employees. On occasion, employees will need extended leaves of absence to address family situations or personal health issues. The federal Family and Medical Leave Act governs a good portion of such absences, and the library's local policy must comply with the federal law. Note should be made of the extent of vacation, bereavement, jury duty, or military leave time available to employees. The policy should state which employees are eligible for paid leave (full-time, part-time salaried, substitute, or hourly employees).

Even if the library uses a consultant to write the first draft of the personnel manual, it is essential that the library hire an attorney to review all personnel policies. Labor law is constantly changing, and careful legal verification of all personnel policies before adoption will save the library time and money in the long run.

The second broad category of personnel policies covers benefits the library offers employees and clarifies which employees will be eligible for full or prorated benefits. Many libraries will offer some prorated benefits to employees working more than half-time but less than full-time. Because the library will be competing for employees with other area libraries and organizations, it behooves the board to gather personnel policies from area libraries. By looking at area policies, the governing board can see what other employers are offering employees and thus put together a benefit package that is competitive.

The types and amount of benefits a library will offer its employees will depend on a combination of factors. Financial resources, library philosophy concerning the quality of staff that it desires, salary competitiveness, and the benefit packages being offered in libraries and businesses in the area must all be considered.

Selecting insurance plans is a daunting task that can be made easier with the help of a knowledgeable insurance agent. A licensed insurance agent or broker will walk the library board or director through all the options so that informed decisions can be made. The agent will research the market to find carriers with competitive pricing and types of plan design.

Most libraries offer some form of health-care insurance, which can be very expensive for the library, but is a benefit that is essential to employees. The policy should state the extent of the coverage. The library might be able to join a professional association, local chamber of commerce, or municipal government to get better rates as part of a larger group. Regardless of the way the library joins a health insurance group, a good plan can be a key factor in attracting employees to the library.

There are two broad categories of health insurance—fee-for-service or managed care. The fee-for-service coverage allows employees to select their health-care professionals and to have those health-care professionals be paid directly by the library's insurance company. The policy may require coinsurance, whereby the employee pays a certain percentage of the bill and the insurance company pays the remainder. The term *managed care* is used to describe three slightly different types of plans—health maintenance organizations (HMOs), preferred provider organizations (PPOs), and point-of-service (POS) plans. Essentially these plans limit the employee to using doctors or facilities that belong to or are approved by the plan. Often the employee's portion of health-care costs is less under a managed care plan than under a fee-for-service plan.

As important as the type of health-care plan being offered is the extent of the coverage. Will the library provide full family coverage or only cover the employee? Will dependent children over the age of nineteen be covered and at whose expense? Are office visits for routine health checks covered? Does the plan provide prescription drugs, dental care, and optical coverage? Most forms of health-care insurance include some co-pay on the employee's part and this can vary quite a bit. Finally, the library board must decide if the employee will be asked to share in the monthly premium or if the library will be paying the full monthly fee.

Disability insurance is offered to many library employees. A library may choose to offer short- or long-term disability insurance or both, which will replace a portion (typically 60 percent) of an employee's income when that employee is incapacitated because of illness or injury. The library can realize significant cost savings by integrating the short-term coverage with the library's sick leave plan. For example, the employee must cover the first thirty days of the disability period by using accrued benefit time (sick time, vacation, personal business, etc.) before short-term coverage is activated. The library's short-term policy might then pick up the time between the second and sixth months of the disability. The library may want to purchase a short-term disability policy or consider budgeting for a self-insurance fund. Long-term disability insurance supplements short-term coverage and typically starts six months after the first day of disability and can continue for the rest of the employee's life. Because the library's exposure on long-term disability can extend for years, it is best for the library to contract with an insurance carrier for long-term disability coverage.

Life insurance is another type of insurance that libraries commonly offer employees. There are two categories of life insurance—term and permanent. Employers are more likely to offer employees term life insurance, because the premiums are less than those associated with permanent life insurance. Under a term life insurance policy, an employee is covered as long as the library employs him or her. Upon the employee's death, his or her beneficiaries receive a death benefit payout, which provides some temporary income replacement.

Retirement and pension plans are available from many libraries. The library might select one of two types of retirement plans. First, there is a defined benefit plan, in which upon retirement the employee is guaranteed a specific monthly income based on salary history and years of service. Each year, the library invests money on behalf of the employee, controls the investment, and bears the risk of that investment. The second type is a defined contribution program, under which the library guarantees a percentage of the employee's salary and the employee makes the investment choices and bears the risk. Under a defined contribution plan, the benefit is portable (i.e., it can be rolled over to an IRA or some other account when the employee leaves the library). These plans include 401 (k) and 403 (b) plans. A defined contribution program makes library budgeting easy because the premium is based on a percentage of annual salary. It also allows the employee full control over the investment of the money, thus relieving the library of fiduciary responsibility.

Regardless of whether or not a retirement plan is offered, the library may want to consider offering employees a deferred compensation program. Deferred compensation programs are not considered retirement plans by the IRS, and employers are not allowed to contribute to deferred compensation plans. Employees are allowed to have pretax dollars withheld from their salary, which are then deposited into IRS-approved 401(k), 403(b), or 457 plans. The money is eligible for distribution after the employee has reached the age of fifty-nine. At that time the employee has the tax liability. In deferred compensation plans, the employee makes all investment decisions and assumes all investment risk.

As the library gets larger, it may consider offering a cafeteria plan that allows employees to redirect a portion of their pretax salary to pay for such expenses as insurance premiums, dependent care, or out-of-pocket medical, dental, and vision care. The library also benefits as these pretax dollars lower the amount of the library's employment taxes (social security and federal unemployment).

Creating personnel policies and selecting benefit packages take a great deal of time, but it is time well spent. Libraries should see what other employers in the area are offering and work with professionals on putting packages together. Attorneys and insurance agents will provide expert guidance in preparing benefit packages that the library may be obligated to provide for its staff for years to come. Careful planning at the beginning can save time and money once the library is in full operation. Good benefits and salaries will put the library in a better position for attracting top-notch employees. A well-thought-out and fair personnel manual will help keep good employees and ensure that all employees are treated equally and fairly.

SERVICE POLICIES

Just as personnel policies describe the relationship between the library and its employees, service policies describe the relationship between the library and its public. Policies are not written in a vacuum. The values, mission, and roles of the library and its parent institutions must be taken into consideration. The community, its needs, and its use of libraries must also be considered.[3]

The introduction to the Clinton-Macomb (Mich.) Public Library's service manual shown in figure 6-2 was adapted from a circulation policy manual from the Montgomery County (Md.) Library. This introduction sets a tone that is seen throughout the entire manual. This policy manual is seen as a guideline for staff, but the staff is empowered, in fact expected, to flex the policies to meet customer needs without hurting the rest of the community.

FIGURE 6-2   Introduction to the Clinton-Macomb Public Library Service Manual

Our service to library customers is based on the values of our organization rather than merely on rules and procedures. We base our service policies on the mission of the Library and the shared organizational values. Certain general concepts of our values-based service differ from a service that is based solely on policies and procedures. These include:

Empowerment. Staff is encouraged to make local decisions that will result in success for library customers. This means that anyone, not just a supervisor, can make an exception to policy or procedure if it provides quality service and is consistent with our organizational values. We know that customers like to have their problems solved by the first staff person with whom they deal. Staff should feel confident and comfortable in solving individual problems. On the other hand, we wish to reassure staff that there are times when it helps to ask the advice of a colleague or supervisor, and such a team approach to problem solving is encouraged.

Consistently Applying Values. With staff making local decisions there is concern about consistency. In a values-based service, it is important that we consistently apply the values of fairness, respect, and quality. Though it is quite possible that the procedural details of how a situation is handled might vary, library customers should feel that we consistently listen carefully and try to meet their individual needs, that we treat them with respect and fairness, and that we strive to do the right thing. We recognize that individual perceptions differ, and that we may need to vary how we deal with a situation based not only on the circumstances, but also the individual perceptions of the customer.

People-Oriented Service. Our focus is on the customer, both internal and external. We recognize that our library users have human needs that go beyond their needs for access to information or reading materials. Users need to feel welcome, and need to know that we care about their needs and concerns. We must be good listeners.

Making Sense to Our Customers and Ourselves. Library policies must make sense to library customers. When we explain policies, we should be able to do it with the confidence that our policies are just, reasonable, and provide the best possible balance of public service. The reasons behind a policy should be easily understood by all, public and staff alike.

No Hassles. Whenever possible, we remove barriers to successful library use. This is true of our policies and procedures, but should be equally true of our individual transactions with library users.

Flexibility and Accommodation. Flexibility means that we should change our service style and approach based on the customer's needs, personality, and disposition. We recognize that we cannot create a policy and procedure to cover every possible course of action in any given situation. Though standard procedures may call for one course of action, a particular situation may call for a creative nonstandard solution. Decisions are based, in part, on careful analysis of each transaction once the information and facts about the customer's situation have been collected. Creativity and resourcefulness are valued. We do what we can do, within the context of certain basic policies, to make things work for our customers.

Fairness. Balancing the needs of the individual with the overall needs of library customers throughout the library district is our goal. The concept of sharing of resources is key. When we make a decision whether or not to make an exception, it will often hinge on the fairness issue. For example, an individual may express a strong need for extra renewal of a borrowed item and offer compelling testimony of that need. In such a situation, we must judge whether offering the additional renewal would deny others access to the item. On the other hand, would denying the exception constitute an unnecessary hassle for the individual? What is fair depends on the particular circumstances in the case.

Learning and Growing. We believe that staff is capable of learning and growing and that they will make mistakes as these concepts are applied. We accept that as part of the process of growth.

Adapted from the Montgomery County (Md.) Department of Public Libraries Circulation Manual.

Service policies typically cover how the public will be allowed to use the library, starting with the most basic information like hours and days of service (see figure 6-3). As public institutions and spaces, public libraries are open to all, and people have to be informed as to which kinds of behavior will be tolerated. The code of conduct or public behavior policy should be carefully reviewed by an attorney to make sure the civil rights of customers are not infringed upon, while allowing the library to have some control over public behavior in the library. Will the library tolerate conversation at normal voice levels or will customers and staff be expected to whisper? How will the library handle unattended children? People sleeping in the library? Homeless people? How will the library deal with disruptive people? Will the police be called or will the staff handle the problem internally? Exactly what is the code of conduct that the library expects the public to follow while using the library? Each of these situations should be discussed, and policy should be developed to help staff manage disruptive situations.

FIGURE 6-3   Service Policies

Public behavior or code of conduct
Circulation and borrowing rules
Materials selection and collection development
Use of library supplies and equipment
Displays and handouts in the library
Public use of library facilities and equipment

A detailed policy should be developed for circulation and borrowing. This policy will include who may borrow materials and the kinds of identification accepted by the library in order to apply for a library card. This policy will detail loan periods, fees for use of materials, and fine schedules used by the library. The library should detail how it will notify people of overdue and lost materials and whether the library will use a collection agency to retrieve long overdue items. This policy also should address the confidentiality of library records. Many states have a law governing access to library records, and the library board and staff must be well informed on what information may or may not be made public. The USA Patriot Act expands law enforcement's access to library records, and library policies must comply with and address USA Patriot Act requests.

A materials selection policy describes how the library selects materials to support its mission. The policy will outline who will select materials and define what criteria those selectors will use in the selection process. Information on the library's acceptance of gifts or weeding of the collection will be included here. This policy is often where a library board might affirm its support of intellectual freedom through the adoption of the American Library Association's *Library Bill of Rights* and the *Freedom to Read Statement.*

In addition to providing access to information through the books and subscriptions, the library also provides information through pamphlets, flyers, programs, and displays. In many cases, the library will take responsibility for developing pamphlets, programs, and displays, but at other times this information may be provided by people and organizations outside the library. The library should consider where nonlibrary-purchased materials will be distributed or displayed and who will approve materials for distribution. As with regular library materials, both sides of controversial issues should get equal exposure. Will people be allowed to solicit signatures on petitions inside the library or on library property? Will nonlibrary programs and brochures be limited to a specific area of the library? These decisions should be included in a specific policy.

Most people understand that library materials like books, magazines, and audiovisual materials can be used in the library and borrowed for home use, but what about library materials and supplies like paper, staplers, pens, and pencils? Should the library make these items freely available? Probably the most controversial issue is public use of the Internet in the library. Again, state and local laws may influence Internet usage, but most libraries adopt an acceptable use policy that dictates the length of time an individual may use Internet terminals or the type of communication that can occur using library equipment. Obviously illegal activity (child pornography, dealing in illicit substances, or harassment of an individual) cannot be tolerated. But will people be allowed to use the library computers and the library facility to conduct their business? File their income taxes? Access chat rooms or send and receive e-mail? Sometimes libraries restrict the use of their equipment for research purposes only. Some libraries use commercial filters to prohibit customers from viewing adult materials or accessing chat rooms or e-mail services. Each library board needs to consider how much leeway it will give to people who want to use library equipment and facilities, and those decisions, based on community needs and library resources, will vary widely from community to community.

The library should detail the way the building may be used by outside organizations and individuals. Many libraries provide meeting room space for the public, and the board should determine how those spaces may be booked and used. Will nonprofit organizations (homeowners' groups, service clubs, churches, and social and political organizations) be charged for room use? Will for-profit businesses be allowed to use the room and, if so, will there be a fee? Will businesses or individuals be allowed to sell merchandise on library property? What equipment will be provided and how will room arrangements be handled? Will food service be allowed? How about registration or admission fees? How frequently can any one individual or organization reserve and use a library meeting room? How far in advance can a room be booked, and will library programs get priority booking for specific spaces? Will smoking be allowed in the building? How about cooking in meeting rooms or eating in the library in general? Will eating and drinking be allowed in specific areas of the library? All of these issues should be discussed and considered in light of existing community resources and library space. All of these services can attract people to the library who might not normally use the library, but without well-thought-out guidelines, the service can cause more ill will than good.

INSURANCE COVERAGE

Personnel and service policies provide the framework for good management and business, but things will happen that fall outside the policy manual and this is when the library needs to have property and liability insurance. The library needs to insure itself in case employees, volunteers, or customers are injured on the job or on library property. The library needs to protect its building, collections, and equipment. And the library needs to protect itself from mismanagement or poor decision making. This type of coverage is provided through property and casualty insurance.

FIGURE 6-4   Insurance Coverage

Business Property Insurance
Boiler and Machinery Insurance
Valuable Papers and Records Insurance
General Liability Insurance
Employee Benefit Liability
Owned-Auto Insurance
Workers' Compensation
Directors' and Officers' Liability
Fidelity Bonds

Again, this is the time to work with a professional insurance agent who can explain each type of insurance coverage (see figure 6-4) and get the library the best rates from the many insurance carriers.

Business property insurance is very similar to the insurance most people have on their homes and protects the library from damage caused by fire, vandalism, earthquakes, and floods. The plans are offered in bits and pieces, so if the library is not at risk for earthquakes or floods, it need not pay for that coverage. Property insurance also covers the library book collection. The library will be asked to provide a dollar value for the collection, which might be available through the library's automated circulation system. The prudent library will insure the collection at the list price, because replacement costs will generally be higher than the materials' original purchase price, and staff time will be needed to rebuild the collection.

Boiler and machinery insurance protects the library's equipment and systems from power surges, lightning, or damage caused by other equipment in the library. Examples of the type of damage covered include water damage to computers from faulty sprinkler systems or broken water pipes, power surges that damage the library's automation or phone system, or surges into the heating and cooling system.

Valuable papers and records insurance covers the library's rare books. Generally the library's book and materials collection will be covered under the general liability policy, but if the library does have expensive special collections, they should be covered separately.

Property insurance policies cover the library's property, but additional coverage should be provided to protect the library from third-party liability suits and management errors. No matter how conscientious the library is, accidents will happen, and *general liability insurance* protects the library from third-party suits related to injuries or damage to personal property. Customers will trip and fall in the library and may be injured. Liability insurance covers claims made by customers or library volunteers. Umbrella policies will extend the library's coverage above and beyond the general liability insurance program.

If the library is responsible for providing employee benefits, it may want to have *employee benefit liability insurance* to cover errors in the administration of the benefit plans. If the library forgets to add an employee to a benefit plan and the employee is unintentionally left uncovered, the library's liability insurance will protect the library.

If the library is going to own vehicles (cars, trucks, or bookmobiles), it will need *owned-auto insurance* to protect the library from financial loss because of legal liability for car-related injuries to others or damage to their property. If an employee is going to use his or her personal car for library business, the library will need hired or nonowned auto insurance. This insurance protects the library from any third-party liability claim against the library and is not meant to cover damage to vehicles.

Workers' compensation laws vary from state to state, but insurance is available to cover employees who are injured or killed while on the job. The benefits will include lost wages and medical care costs. Additional coverage may be considered for employees injured in situations that occur while they are not working. This additional coverage is called accidental death and dismemberment.

Governing library boards should be making decisions regarding library actions and policies after careful research and discussion, but at times a wrong decision will be made or cases of mismanagement will arise. When this happens, *directors'* (trustees, not library directors) *and officers' insurance* will protect the board. The library is also protected when poor employment practices occur, such as in a wrongful discharge case.

Libraries handle large amounts of money each year: tax revenues, overdue fines, and allocations from other governmental units. Even with careful internal controls and annual audits, the library should have insurance to cover the mismanagement of financial resources. A *fidelity bond* protects the library from dishonest or fraudulent acts of employees, such as embezzlement, fraud, or theft of money.

This may sound like a lot of insurance, but the library needs to protect its assets and the public's interest. A good insurance agent will review the library's coverage each year to make sure that the coverage is adequate and that the library administration is familiar with the coverage purchased. It is very important that the library director is familiar with the coverage available. Significant amounts of money can be saved if the appropriate insurance is in place, but simply having the insurance is not enough. The library must remember to submit claims when incidents occur.

CONCLUSION

As with any business, good planning is essential for success. Adoption of appropriate policies and the purchase of appropriate insurance are important tools that protect the library, library employees, customers, and volunteers. Good policies and insurance plans are part of the library's business plan. Librarians are not often trained in these areas, so it is essential that the library consult with attorneys, auditors, and insurance agents to make sure the public's interests are protected.

NOTES

1. Sandra Nelson and June Garcia, *Creating Policies for Results: From Chaos to Clarity* (Chicago: ALA, 2003).
2. Jeanette Larson and Herman L. Totten, *Model Policies for Small and Medium Public Libraries* (New York: Neal-Schuman, 1998), 11–13.
3. PLA Policy Manual Committee, *PLA Handbook for Writers of Public Library Policies* (Chicago: ALA, 1993), 2.

7

Planning for the Long Term

by Charlaine Ezell

A library without a long-range plan is like a group of people who pile into a car and then leave town without any clear idea—or any agreement—on where they are going or what they are going to do once they get there. Yet many library boards operate this way. They may make decisions about the library for the short term, but a board of trustees will be more productive by setting a direction for long-term library growth and development over the course of several years. With a long-range plan in place, it becomes easier during board meetings for trustees to make sound, considered decisions on a short-term basis and reach agreement among all the trustees on these decisions.

In this chapter, we look at the reasons the library board should have a long-range plan, the types of planning models a board can consider, information the board will need in order to begin planning, and how a library board can use its plan as a guide for board business.

CHARLAINE EZELL is president of The Extra Edge, a training and consulting firm specializing in public libraries. Charlaine is a certified trainer and professional librarian with a background in administration, management, public relations, reference, children's services, and library marketing. A highly popular workshop presenter and facilitator, she has worked in almost every state in the United States. She is the author of *To Hew against the Grain: Influence Strategies to Effect Innovation* and numerous research studies on library marketing, funding, and planning.

REASONS FOR PLANNING

The inducements to create a long-range plan for the library come from many sources. Often, the need to remodel or expand space will precipitate planning. One of the most common reasons is the need for a better or an expanded facility. While it may be obvious that the library "needs more space," the first thing the builder or architect will want to know is how that additional space is to be used. A long-range plan for the library facility will answer this question as well as go beyond the addition of square footage for materials or reader space to the implications of staffing, program activities, and new services inside that space.

At other times, the need for a long-range plan is driven by the community's governing authority, who may ask the library board to prepare a plan that puts the library in alignment with other governmental departments or agencies. Cities, counties, villages, and townships are now creating long-range plans for their communities and want their public libraries' growth to be a cohesive part of the whole plan.

It is no secret that the service programs of many public libraries are planned "from the director's head"—that is, the chief administrator has a clear picture in mind of what he or she wants for the library and guides the library board to make decisions based on that personal vision. Although this type of planning is economical, it puts the responsibility for planning in the director's lap when by law and by rights, it should be in the library board's.

Some directors are aware of this and shy away from taking on the board's responsibility for planning. They are uncomfortable making decisions with long-term consequences for the library and doing so with little guidance from their boards. Sometimes director frustration will spur the trustees to consider creating a long-range plan.

Having a long-range plan in place is an achievement for a library board that will pay off handsomely in the library's future. A long-range plan clearly allows the board to set priorities so that everybody knows what the purpose of the library should be, and it helps to realign services. It helps the board determine what policies are needed and how they should be enforced. It saves valuable time in board meetings and discussions because the board has a template, or criteria, for evaluating courses of action. A plan for action is energizing. It ignites people. People work harder, and better, when they know what they are working for and why. It directs the administrator's and staff's activities on a day-to-day basis. It tells them what they should be doing and why. A strategic plan also guides the budget. It influences the board's decisions about how much money it will need to run a library and if it is spending that money on the right things. There are also legal and ethical reasons to have a plan for the library: Nonprofit boards of trustees have been held up for public scrutiny because of their expending public monies without a long-range plan to justify their financial decisions.

The best plans for libraries are community-based. That is, not only are the trustees who represent the community engaged in the planning process, but the residents, governing officials, and target audiences or constituencies are also actively involved in the plan for the library. The opinions of its residents, especially those who are library users, are actively solicited and listened to and their support for the library's future encouraged. The library is a public institution; the public should most certainly be deeply involved in its future.

The following planning models all have components of community-based planning implicit in them.

TYPES OF PLANS AND PLANNING MODELS

There are all kinds of plans and all kinds of planning models. Most of them have a vision and mission statement, long-range goals, specific objectives, and activities to meet those objectives, although the complexity of all of these varies.

Long-range plans span several years, usually three to five although some are longer. Short-range plans are based on a long-range plan and break down the ambitious and far-reaching goals of the latter into activities that usually last for one year. Traditionally, long- and short-range plans were predicated on events, progress, and the history of the organization and usually inspired confidence that any changes made in the organization would be similar to those made in the past.

Strategic plans were developed because at some point, a library might have to consider downsizing or plateauing as well as growing and expanding, and these shifts might be dramatic or sudden. Such shifts had to be reflected in the plan for the future.

Scenario planning is a planning model used very effectively when a library is uncertain of its future, such as when it faces a budget crisis or a sudden change in governmental structure or community demographics. In this type of planning model, the library board examines those factors, or driving forces, over which it has no control and then examines the issues that are hard to predict or difficult to imagine. The library board "rehearses the implications" by describing how the driving forces might plausibly affect the uncertainties in a number of possible scenarios. The discussions about these are usually drawn in a matrix where participants are able to see how shifting patterns of events will influence the library's future. From these scenarios, a written plan can be developed that allows the library to realign itself as the future unfolds, thus creating a nimble organization keeping pace with changing events.

Another type of planning is based on a way of thinking called *continuous improvement*. In this case, a library is constantly monitoring and assessing the usefulness and effectiveness of its services and introduces new services or discontinues outdated or unpopular ones without a formal, specific starting date. The library is reorganizing and reengineering as time moves along. A specific example of this type of planning is the library board that reads all comments each month that come from the patrons' suggestion box and decides to act on suggestions it finds there. Although this type of library planning may not appear to be either ambitious or longsighted, it can be very effective, especially if the library has based the changes made on a clear statement of purpose and a clear direction for the future.

COMPONENTS OF A PLAN

A good plan will have several components: a mission statement, core values, goals, and priorities for service. It may also have a vision statement. The plan will clearly state the principles that drive the library service program and will reflect a deep understanding of the kind of work the library should do. It may also have an implementation plan appended, with specific activities, stakeholders, timetables, and budgetary amounts slotted in so that the goals and objectives are achieved.

These days, technologies and patron expectations are changing so rapidly that it is almost impossible to develop a plan that can realistically cycle through more than four years. More important to the future of your library is a strategic plan, one that lets you focus on the future instead of the present and the past and be flexible about reaching your goals as the future unfolds. It is hard to plan for a nonprofit organization more than three to five years into the future, but it is very important to set ambitious goals and then continually check to see if the priorities for the library are addressed and the goals are being met.

INFORMATION NEEDED FOR PLANNING

No decisions about something as crucial as a library's future should be made impulsively. Yet many public libraries fail to consider what they will need to know in order to plan effectively.

Let us assume that you are going on vacation. You have some information about this already: what you might do or where you might go. You may decide to stay at home or to go on a trip. Even if you plan on staying home from work for a week, you usually have several activities in mind. You have to take into consideration the amount of time and money you have and how you want to spend both. Some of this information will be qualitative—that is, your feelings and preferences about what will be fun. Some of this will be quantitative—specific data on how long your vacation is or how much money you have to spend.

A library board collects similar information, or data, when it begins to plan. Data collection is the process of gathering and analyzing statistics, percentages, and other numerical information (quantitative data). It is also the gathering and analyzing of subjective data, such as comments from users and nonusers (qualitative data). For most libraries, we would suggest gathering both types of data before the board begins a formal plan. Each has advantages and disadvantages.

Most public libraries commonly collect data through "counts and tallies," such as the number of print and nonprint materials checked out each year, or the number of story times sponsored or reference questions answered. These counts may be useful information for state aid reports, but they do not always reveal what the general public feels about the library's services, nor do they give information about users' priorities for library services. That kind of data is best collected through surveys, mystery shopper experiences, telephone polls, personal interviews, focus groups, and patron observation and tracking.

Before collecting data, a library board should be very clear what it wants to learn from them. The nature of the questions should drive the decision to use a certain method. Each of the preceding methods has its advantages and disadvantages. The outcome should be that the library board has reliable, accurate, and valid data on which to base their discussions and decisions.

The process of getting the right information is best left to professionals. Just as the board would not expect the library staff to write the books in its collection or repair the leaks in the roof, neither should the trustees expect the staff to be professionals at data instrument design and data collection. In the interest of saving money, many boards require that the library director or staff spend a great deal of time doing this work. Quite often this results in using a poorly designed survey form, failing to ask the right questions, collecting the wrong information, or improperly analyzing the results. For this reason, we heartily recommend hiring professionals, such as statisticians, survey designers, and certified focus group facilitators, to collect the data that the library would not usually collect as part of its regular counts and tallies.

FACTORS TO CONSIDER IN THE PLANNING PROCESS

All libraries are different; so also are their planning processes. No two will be alike. Some library boards incorporate planning as part of their usual board business each quarter or month. Some hold an annual board retreat, where for one or two days the library board engages in intensive discussions and reflective thinking about the future of the library in a setting and for an extended period of time that is usually not possible during a regular monthly board meeting.

Some library boards delegate planning to a subcommittee of the board. Others insist that all the trustees participate. Some library trustees invite other participants to be part of a library planning team: the director, key staff, city or county planners, leaders of community groups, other librarians, and the like. Including these people on a planning team helps to educate the rest of the community, through its opinion leaders, about the needs and issues affecting the library.

Some boards hire a professional meeting facilitator to guide their discussions, ensure that minority opinions are heard, and keep to the agenda set for the retreat. Some of these individuals are professional librarians as well as certified meeting facilitators. They have an added advantage: They speak "library" and can help library board members and directors see what is on the horizon for public library development—trends in the field, levels of service, different types of library programs and services, and ways to reach community residents.

Planners meet for the purpose of drafting a plan, with a clear mission, defined roles, and priorities for service. They review the data that were collected and discuss the implications. They itemize the problems facing the library as a whole and review challenges to the administration or management that they want to solve in the next few years. They look at trends in the field of librarianship. They make lists of shortcomings, problems, snags, and obstacles for the various services and programs the library currently offers. They consider what new services the library might provide and whether and when to discontinue services that are no longer popular.

They should review the library's mission, or purpose, in the community. Many library boards realize that there simply is not enough money, staff, time, or reason to offer everybody everything. They know they must focus on what the library's purpose is, what its role in the community should be, and how best to achieve it. This becomes the library's mission. For some libraries, the concept of a mission is new and they see no reason for one. For others, stating the mission helps set a direction for making decisions about the day-to-day activities of the staff. It can be an energizing force that focuses public as well as staff attention on the library.

Whatever the library's purpose, its mission should be ambitious and positive. It should be brief enough for people to remember. If it is too long, then no one will remember it, and if people can't remember it, they certainly can't implement it.

The written plan for the library can take many forms. Some are formal, with goals, objectives, activities, and implementation timetables. Some are lists of collective details based on past practices. Other written plans are more informal—a short list of "things to do" in the coming year or years.

When the plan has been written as a final draft, it should come to the board for review. We suggest that the entire board, if it has not participated in the planning process, review the plan and discuss it, so that every trustee is absolutely clear on what it means and what it implies. This type of communication is absolutely crucial. Although the current library trustees may expect to get a written statement of priorities, they also get consensus on what the library's priorities are and how they will be met. Furthermore, as new board members are elected or appointed, they can enter the setting more effectively and participate more fully if they understand the long-range plan and the board decisions that were made in its light.

It is the responsibility of the library director to implement the plan. He or she will be working with the library staff to do so. In order to give maximum flexibility to the library and its stakeholders, we suggest that the library board adopt the library's mission, values, goals, and objectives as stated or revised but not the activities per se, for these may change as the plan unfolds. To insist that the director and staff adhere to the activities that were prescribed even a year ago is to invite disaster. Furthermore, it puts the board in the position of micromanaging and wastes trustees' time in board meetings concentrating on implementation concerns, time that would be better spent discussing policy or strategic issues and ensuring that there are adequate resources to accomplish the plan.

The board should formally approve the plan as an official and appropriate act of business, and this should be recorded in the minutes as such. There is a deep psychological value in having every trustee sign the final plan. Once the long-range plan is approved, we suggest that a copy be included in every board member's notebook, inserted in the front cover so that it can be found easily. Certainly, the plan should be made public, usually with an announcement in the media or at a public hearing. The plan itself should be readily available to the library patrons, for it can be used as a fund-raising and marketing tool.

USING THE PLAN AS A GUIDE FOR BOARD BUSINESS

The board includes "planning" in its regular activities in several ways. First and foremost, the library board should use its meetings as a time to review the plan and consider strategic directions for the library as a whole, to guide their discussions of policy formation and development.

The trustees can use the long-range plan in hiring a director with the specific skills and experience needed to achieve that plan. The library board can use the plan to assess the director's performance, usually on an annual basis. The board can use the plan to prepare its presentation to funding sources to ensure that there are adequate financial resources to meet the objectives in the plan. As with the budget, the board should develop or review library policies to be certain they are in alignment with the goals in the plan.

The board can use the plan as the foundation for debating board business. We suggest verbally beginning each board meeting with the mission statement. The library's mission and goals should be readily known to all the trustees. In this way, the plan is an agenda-setting guide for board meetings. Furthermore, concentrating on the library's mission and goals reduces the amount of time spent on minor details, side issues, and one or two individuals' agendas.

The trustees should also make a "planning review" part of their business and do this for the purpose of monitoring the plan. They may ask the director to develop a service plan, also called an implementation plan or an annual plan, with activities and step-by-step procedures for completing each objective in the long-range plan to be completed in a given year. Appropriate staff members are assigned to carry out the various objectives and activities.

While personnel are being assigned to carry out individual activities of the plan, it may be helpful to develop a chart or worksheet for each objective that lists each of the activities, the person(s) responsible for implementing it, the resources needed to achieve it, and the starting and ending dates. At the same time, the director might ask, "What impact will this have on existing budgets, the facility, and the collection or other resources?" and list those on the chart as well.

When this outline or chart is shared by the staff, every staff member and every trustee can see where his or her job fits into the library's overall mission and how his or her work contributes to the long-term goals of the library. This chart is prepared every year, so that the work of the first year flows into the second, the second into the third, and so on.

The library board, through the director, should ask for and receive regular and full reports on progress being made on the individual parts of the plan. It might do this quarterly or semiquarterly. If no progress is made, or if alternate strategies to accomplish some objective have to be devised, the board needs to know this. If obstacles to any of the activities in the plan crop up, the board should certainly discuss them and brainstorm ideas for how to implement the solutions, but the actual work of implementation is the staff's responsibility.

The trustees should evaluate the goals in the long-range plan regularly. For the most part, these goals should not be changed, but should be functional for at least three or four years. The mission should be reviewed annually, but should not change significantly.

CONCLUSION

Planning for the library's future is the essential purpose of the library board of trustees. There are numerous reasons for the library board to have a long-range plan, and several planning models are available to choose from. The long-range plan drives every other board responsibility: hiring and assessing the director's performance, ensuring adequate financial and community support, marketing, and allocating resources. Components of library plans are as distinctive as their libraries and may fill single sheets of paper or lengthy, bound documents of missions, goals, and objectives couched in formal planning terms. The types of data that feed into a library plan are essential to making sound decisions about the library's future. A planning process can be an exercise in thoughtful discussion and consensus building about the library's future, saving time and creating a venue for more fruitful discussion and decisions on the part of the library board.

8

Participating in Cooperative Arrangements

Sarah Ann Long, president of the American Library Association (1999–2000), chose "Libraries Build Community" as the theme of her presidential year. She believes that to be effective, librarians must collaborate and form partnerships and alliances with individuals and organizations that share common goals.[1] This willingness to partner and form alliances goes back to the very beginnings of American public libraries.

The first libraries in America were formed for the purpose of sharing books with other people in the immediate community. Public money was used to build a collection of materials that community members could borrow from the library. As communities grew and library usage increased, it became apparent that a single library would not be able to meet all the information needs of its community.

BORROWING AGREEMENTS

One of the first cooperative arrangements between libraries was for the purpose of sharing resources. Librarians began to develop some cooperative agreements that would provide specific materials to customers without actually requiring each library to purchase specialized books. Interlibrary loan, deposit collections, and reciprocal borrowing agreements were the services that emerged to meet special and, in most cases, temporary needs for specialized materials.

Interlibrary loan is an agreement that allows libraries to borrow and loan materials to other libraries worldwide. When a customer requests an item his or her local library does not own, the local library may offer to borrow the material on the customer's behalf from another library. Typically, before placing the request, a library will search a large database to determine which libraries in the world own the item. Once the material is located, the library can request a loan from the owner library. Even though the library places the request on behalf of the customer, the loan is from library to library. In many cases, the material is loaned free of charge for three to four weeks. In some cases, the lending library may charge the borrowing library a handling fee. This fee may be passed on to the customer or may be absorbed by the borrowing library. When the material is received at the borrowing library, the customer is notified and can then borrow the material from his or her local library. The customer also returns the material to his or her local library, which then returns it to the lending or owning library.

Interlibrary loan service has some inherent limitations. First, the request is made for a specific item. The customer's home library identifies a specific title that is needed and then locates libraries owning that title. The borrowing library decides which library it wishes to ask for the material. This decision may be based on delivery systems available between the libraries, on costs or use restrictions imposed by the lending library, or on existing agreements between libraries. The customer requesting the material is not granted any rights of access to the owning library and, in fact, may have to abide by special loan restrictions, such as in-library use only or a shorter loan period. In addition, access to certain formats (magazines, microforms, DVDs, videos, CDs) may be denied. The lending library has the right to pass on any interloan request. The lending library may decide not to interloan new materials or materials that are on wait lists for local customers. The important fact of interlibrary loan is that the transaction is between the two libraries, not between an individual and a remote library. Interlibrary loan is totally focused on the lending of specific items and does not include access to other library services, such as reference service, program attendance, or the ability to place items on hold.

A second type of cooperative agreement between libraries is the *deposit collection*. On occasion, larger libraries are willing to loan a portion of their collection to another library for an extended period. A regional library may have more storage space and may maintain collections of books of special interest (holidays, leaf and insect identification, state or country history materials), which are loaned to smaller libraries for extended periods of three to four months. When the demand in the smaller library is over, the entire deposit collection is sent back to the larger library for storage. Smaller libraries may be able to ask larger libraries to loan a selection of books on a special topic to meet a temporary local need, such as a special school assignment, book discussion, or community project. Once the local need has been met, the materials can be returned to the larger library. On occasion, public libraries may create deposit collections for classrooms, nursing homes, or waiting rooms in local social or health service facilities. The deposit collection typically has a longer loan period than an interlibrary loan and consists of multiple items. Like interloan, deposit collections are loans between institutions and typically are not made to individuals.

The third type of agreement does focus on the individual. *Reciprocal borrowing agreements* allow individuals to borrow materials directly from a library that is not their home library. The agreement itself is made between two or more libraries on behalf of their individual customers. The difference between interlibrary loan and deposit collections and this type of service is that the individual is allowed to walk into a library other than his or her own and borrow materials without the involvement of the home library. Some states support statewide reciprocal borrowing programs where residents can walk in and use any library in their state. In some states, libraries are compensated on a per-loan basis for offering reciprocal borrowing services, while in other states, libraries may participate with no compensation and on a completely voluntary basis. Even in a state without a statewide program, reciprocal borrowing may be present on a more local basis. Residents may be permitted to use libraries and borrow materials outside the local community or county. The reciprocity may be as simple as an agreement to share collections between two libraries or between libraries in the same library system.

Rules will vary with each reciprocal borrowing program. Customers may or may not be expected to return the material directly to the lending library. In other cases, the material may be returned to the customer's home library or to any library in the area. There may or may not be any customer fees associated with the use of a reciprocal borrowing program. Some libraries may charge a nominal fee per item. Some may limit the borrowing to print items only or may limit the nonresident's use of the lending library's facility and services (no more than two books at a time, no Internet access, no program attendance, no interlibrary loan, etc.). The extent of the library's generosity will depend upon the agreement negotiated by the participating libraries.

Interlibrary loan, deposit collections, and reciprocal borrowing agreements generally do not account for a high percentage of any library's usage.

These services are more expensive and time-consuming than regular loans from a library, but they offer a great service to the customer and to libraries. Individuals doing specialized research may need a book for a short period that no one else in the community will ever need. It may be more cost-effective for the library to borrow the item for the customer than to purchase it for a onetime use. It may even be faster to borrow an item than to purchase it and add it to the collection. Deposit collections allow libraries to expand and shrink their collections to meet short-term needs of customers. By rotating books using a deposit collection agreement, libraries that are short on space need not be short on resources. Reciprocal borrowing agreements allow customers to browse another library's collection and personally select the material they need from a library other than their home library. Specialized agreements to meet specialized needs are excellent mechanisms for expanding access to library materials on a cooperative basis.

COOPERATIVES, CONSORTIA, SYSTEMS, AND NETWORKS

Formal agreements to extend borrowing privileges are just one form of cooperation that is prevalent in libraries today. Librarians are eager to share their skills, talents, information, collections, and experiences and have banded together to create other opportunities for sharing discounts, equipment, and services. As with borrowing agreements, some states strongly support library cooperatives, systems, or networks with state funding. These formal consortia often have governing boards and are held accountable for the way in which the state money or cooperative money is spent. In addition to a governing board, there may be a board of librarians that participates in the governance of the organization or assists in the selection of services or projects to be shared and developed.

These consortia can offer a wide array of services. It is common for consortia to operate a delivery or courier service that facilitates the movement of library materials between member libraries. The consortia can easily move books and other library materials between its member libraries on a daily or weekly basis. Delivery service also supports reciprocal borrowing agreements. When a customer uses a reciprocal borrowing agreement, he or she will borrow material from a library other than his or her home library. That material may be returned to the customer's home library, which will ship it back to the owning library, thus saving the customer a return trip to the more remote library.

Consortia often negotiate discounts with library book and periodical vendors based on the total buying power of the consortium. Negotiated discounts on the processing of those orders or free shipping from the vendor to members of the consortium are also common. The discount packages offered will vary from consortium to consortium, but generally the discounts offered to consortia tend to be larger than the discounts offered to individual libraries by as much as 5 to 10 percent.

In addition to discounts on the purchase of print and nonprint materials, the consortium may be able to negotiate discounts on office and library supplies, equipment, repair and rebinding of damaged books, and printing or delivery services. The types of shared discounts that could be negotiated are limited only by the imagination of the libraries involved in the consortium.

Offering information or entertainment programs for adults and children is another area in which systems can help individual libraries. The creation of speakers' bureaus or lists of good entertainers (magicians, musical performance groups, live animal shows, authors, etc.) are often created by groups of libraries. The list may include fees, audience reaction, and special equipment or staging needed by the performers. Libraries typically offer summer reading programs for children and, more recently, adults, and speakers and entertainers have become integral to those reading programs. An added advantage is that speaker fees may be lower if libraries cluster their programs to save travel time and expense for the speaker.

Automation has become a popular shared resource among libraries. Selecting and installing an automated computer system for inventory control and for materials check-in and checkout is a daunting task. By working with a group of other libraries, it is possible to get a wider evaluation of the automation product and to take advantage of another library's experience with automation. The technical staff needed to manage such a system may be beyond the means of a single library, but very affordable when the cost is spread among a group of libraries.

The range of services, amounts of discounts, and level of cooperation will vary widely from one system to another. Experience has shown that large and small libraries can benefit by sharing resources, experience, and technology. Exactly how that is defined in each state, region, or county will vary depending on the needs of the participating libraries; however, collaboration efforts between libraries always provide an enhanced service for the customer.

SHARED FACILITIES

When public library trustees are deciding where to locate the library, they may want to consider joint facilities with other organizations or libraries. The most typical kinds of cooperative service arrangements occur between like libraries (public and public, school and school, academic and academic), but there is a considerable amount of interest in different types of libraries sharing space. The San Jose (Calif.) Public Library and the San Jose State University Library built a new library building that combines the resources, services, and staff of the public and university libraries, giving the community greater access to information and technology. The new building provides the growth space needed in both libraries as well as some shared spaces, such as a checkout desk, a cafe, program and meeting rooms, an information and directions desk, computer instruction and lab areas, study areas, adult reference desks, and combined collections of adult nonfiction, periodicals, and audiovisual materials. All materials owned by either the city or the university are accessible to all users of the library. Noncirculating materials are shelved together (reference, periodicals, etc.). Circulating materials are shelved separately but are available for checkout to all users.

Another approach to shared services can be seen between public libraries and school libraries. School and public libraries often serve the same populations in the same service area and both institutions are publicly supported. It is easy to see why some communities have combined the two services. The joint library may be housed in a school facility and may share public library and media center staff. The school library might remain open after school hours to serve adults, provide access to the school's collection, and provide a family-friendly community space that is close to where people live. Factors leading to successful cooperative agreements between school media centers and public libraries include a shared vision of library service to diverse populations, agreement on a joint governance structure, policies and procedures, and adequate funding.[2]

Although on the surface shared-facility libraries are appealing, they also offer many challenges. The first difficulty comes to light in comparing the mission of different types of libraries. Each type of library (public, school, academic, and special) serves a specific audience. Public libraries serve the entire community from womb to tomb, while school libraries focus on providing materials at specific grade levels and that match the curriculum offered by that school. Academic libraries support formal education programs offered in community colleges, four-year institutions, and universities, and they collect and make available materials that support graduate education and research. Special libraries serve their governing institution, whether that is a hospital, a corporation, a law firm, or an industrial plant. Since libraries select materials and design services and programs to best serve their community, the combining of various types of libraries can lead to a loss of focus for each library. These different missions and collections make it difficult to serve the public library customer while serving the clientele of another type of library. Public libraries must be cognizant of these differences before entering into agreements to share facilities or staff with other types of libraries.

The library's physical location can be problematic. Public libraries are best situated in highly visible and accessible areas, such as major shopping or traffic areas of the community. Schools, on the other hand, tend to be in more residential areas of the community. University libraries tend to be located in the center of the university campus. And the special library, because of the possible confidential nature of its resources, is often in a nonpublic area of its governing institution. Finding a location that works well for two different types of libraries can be done, but only if libraries are aware of the needs of the other partner.

Staffing and funding of a shared library can be problematic. Issues related to unions, certification, supervision, and evaluation all need to be thoroughly discussed before creating a shared library. Other questions that warrant substantive discussion are: Who will be responsible for the operation of the physical building? How will the library materials be selected and weeded? What is the appropriate funding mix to operate the shared facility?

Shared facilities and staff may be appropriate, but much thought and preparation are required before opening a shared facility to ensure that the interests of both institutions, the public library and its partner, are protected. It may benefit two mature institutions or may be a tool to help start a small or young library. The relationship may not last forever, and the contract in a sense becomes a prenuptial agreement for the new institution.

PARTNERSHIPS WITH OTHER ORGANIZATIONS

Sometimes a library may want to partner with nonlibrary organizations to meet special service needs. Cafes, business centers, art galleries, literacy programs, and freenets are examples of partnerships that have been successful for public libraries.[3] In these cases, the library may not have the expertise to operate the service and may decide to contract with a local business or community organization. In the case of a partnership between a public library and a for-profit business, the business may be required to pay rent or to return a portion of the revenue generated by the service offered in the library. The Roseville (Minn.) Public Library contracted for coffee shop management with Dunn Brothers Coffee, a Minnesota-based company operating coffee shops in the Twin Cities region. The county signed a five-year lease agreement with Dunn Brothers that paid the library $41,000 in the first year and escalated by 5 percent in each of the next four years. After a remodeling of the library's check-in and checkout area, the 1,800-square-foot coffee shop was constructed. The coffee shop, which is open before the library opens for public service, has been operational since April 17, 1997.[4] The library's customers can now enjoy some light refreshments while they read or study, and the coffee shop has the added benefit of being part of a destination location— the library.

Partnerships between a public library and a nonprofit organization are far more common, particularly between public libraries and 501(c)3 organizations like the Friends of the Library. Many Friends groups operate gift shops or bookshops or conduct other fund-raising activities for the benefit of the library. The Rochester Hills (Mich.) Public Library has a successful gift shop that raises tens of thousands of dollars for the library each year. In addition to the store, the Friends of the Rochester Hills Public Library conducts multiple book sales, a holiday home tour, and a wine tasting fund-raiser each year. These events raise $50,000 or more annually for the library.[5]

Partnerships can generate revenue for the library, increase services within the library, help the public become more aware of the library, and attract new volunteers and library supporters. With careful planning, both the outside organization and the library can benefit.

CONCLUSION

Whether through tried-and-true arrangements like interlibrary loan, reciprocal borrowing, consortia memberships, or innovative facility sharing, public libraries will benefit by becoming partners with other institutions. Public libraries can maintain their independence, while gaining strength through new partnerships. However, there are times and situations when cooperation is not recommended. Thoughtful negotiation and planning can help avoid difficult situations and, as in any successful partnership, both parties have to gain by the relationship. With careful planning, cooperation, and patience, partnerships can be a way to enhance and expand public library services and facilities.

NOTES

1. Kathleen de la Peña McCook, *A Place at the Table: Participating in Community Building* (Chicago: ALA, 2000), vii.
2. School Library Media Research and Shirley A. Fitzgibbons, *School and Public Library Relationships: Essential Ingredients in Implementing Educational Reforms and Improving Student Learning* (U.S. Department of Education). Available at www.ala.org/ aasl/SLMR/vol3/relationships/relationships.html. Accessed 17 November 2002.
3. Sherry Lynch, *The Librarian's Guide to Partnerships* (Fort Atkinson, Wis.: Highsmith, 1999).
4. Coffee shop in the Roseville Library [home page of the Ramsey County (Minn.) Public Library, Roseville]. Available at http://www.ramsey.lib.mn.us/library/ dunn.htm. Accessed 10 November 2002.
5. Friends of the Library [home page of the Rochester Hills (Mich.) Public Library]. Available at www.rhpl.org/Friends.html. Accessed 10 November 2002.

9

Building the Perfect Library

Books, bodies, and buildings are the three main components in any public library project. Books may have been the first materials to be put in a library, but today's library goes far beyond a mere print collection and includes materials in a variety of formats. The "bodies" part of the library recipe generally refers to the staff—a combination of librarians and technical and support staff. The building becomes the most visible image of the library in the community and sometimes the most controversial component of the library.

NEEDS ASSESSMENT

The first challenge is to determine exactly how much space will be needed to provide adequate library service in the community and where that space should be located. This is best accomplished by conducting a formal needs assessment.

A needs assessment will open the door to community discussion on the library. It will look at existing community library services and resources and identify projected library needs. It will identify exactly what kind of facility the library should have and will lay the foundation for the building program statement.

A library needs assessment is a foundation for the building process. It answers the following questions: What size and type of materials collections will be needed in twenty years? What kinds of meeting and conference rooms are projected? How have staff office and workstation space needs changed? What are the library's plans for automation? Once the needed services are identified, some preliminary space planning can begin.[1] This information is gathered in very general terms in order to determine the amount of space needed to provide the best library service possible for the community.

The library board, director, and community planners can conduct the needs assessment themselves or may they hire a library planning consultant to collect and analyze the information. The library consultant's wider experience with other libraries will speed the process along, and the consultant can suggest areas in need of further consideration or new areas for the library building committee to consider and explore. The use of a library consultant will also lend credibility to the needs assessment and will aid the library in marketing and presenting the final report to the community.

The needs assessment will discuss current community demographics and projected population growth both in terms of numbers and locations. Such factors as age distribution of residents, income, education, housing trends and options, and local transportation and individual mobility must all be considered in terms of the provision of library service. This information will contribute to the decision to support a single library outlet or multiple service outlets, such as branches, reading centers, or bookmobiles. The demographic analysis will point toward the types of services the library should provide and the type and amount of space necessary to provide those services.

SITE SELECTION

Once the needs assessment is complete, the library board is ready to discuss the location of the proposed library. Site selection, whether in a rented space, existing space purchased for library use, or an area with potential for new construction, can be the most controversial and political part of the library construction process. Every resident wants to be near the library, but no one wants the library in his or her backyard. The library must be easy to access from major thoroughfares and highly visible in the community, but finding a site that meets those needs and is at the same time affordable can be difficult.

Over the years several models have been used for public library siting. Some have focused on the library in retail centers, while others have endorsed the idea of locating the library in municipal and governmental centers. Some models feature a decentralized library with multiple branches, while others consolidate services and resources in a single outlet.[2]

Even if the library already has or is in a building, this facility should be evaluated in terms of the community's future needs. It may be well sited for the present, but not large enough to accommodate expansion. The building may need such extensive remodeling and renovation that it would be more cost-effective to move to a new site. This type of analysis and appraisal will also be included in the needs assessment.

The board may decide to rent space or to purchase an existing building or to build an entirely new library. All of these options have advantages. In a growing community, the population center may not be stabilized. Perhaps the growth of the community began in one centralized downtown area and is now expanding outward. A branch in rental space in the established portion of the community might be appropriate at the present time, while a more permanent structure in a more centralized area could be considered more appropriate once growth has stabilized throughout the community. Even if the library board decides to rent space in the area with the largest concentration of people, the library trustees will still want to consider land purchase for future growth of the library.

The needs assessment report should project the community's development, and, while vacant land is still available, the library may want to purchase a site for future library expansion. Typically, the prices for vacant land are less in the early life of a community, and as a nonprofit, municipal organization, the library is not liable for property tax if the property is to be used for library purposes in the future. This same principle is used in school districts that typically own vacant land for future school needs. If projections for community growth change, or if the financial situation changes, the library can always sell the property.

The library board may use a realtor to locate property or may decide to look for property and negotiate a rental or purchase agreement on its own. Since many local zoning ordinances allow public libraries in a variety of areas (residential, office, commercial, or industrial), the library will have many options. Shopping for a building or property should be done discreetly so the prices are not inflated when sellers realize the possibilities of having public funding available for the purchase. Library trustees also may accept gifts, such as land or buildings. The donation of such property is tax deductible and this may be appealing to sellers.

When purchasing property, the library board must consider several aspects. The board can create a matrix that will help compare various site options (see figure 9-1 for an example). The board should consult with an architect, an engineer, and a landscape specialist to get an accurate analysis.

FIGURE 9-1 Site Evaluation

Criteria	Weight	Maple Road	Civic Center	Downtown	Existing
Accessibility	20	54	40	76	40
Access from Thoroughfares	10	3	2	3	2
Automobile Travel Time	8	3	2	3	2
Pedestrian Access	2	0	2	1	2
Site Capacity	20	60	50	60	10
Usable Site Area	6	3	2	3	1
Parking	6	3	3	3	0
Configuration	4	3	4	3	1
Expansion Capacity	4	3	1	3	0
Visibility	12	31	29	36	36
Building Placement Potential	5	2	3	3	3
Road Frontage	5	3	2	3	3
Traffic Volumes	2	3	2	3	3
Demographic Patterns	10	20	15	20	23
Center of Population	5	2	2	2	2
Center of User Group	3	2	1	2	3
Geographic Center	2	2	1	2	2
Neighborhood Compatibility	10	15	25	20	30
Adjacent Land Uses	5	2	2	2	3
Development Quality	5	1	3	2	3
Image/Visual Quality	6	22	30	12	22
Area Identity/Landmarks	4	3	3	3	3
Natural Site Amenities	2	1	3	0	1
On-Site Views	2	1	3	0	2
Off-Site Views	2	3	3	0	2
Physical Geography	9	13	27	5	18
Topography, Soils, Vegetation	5	1	3	1	2
Microclimate	4	2	3	0	2

(continued)

FIGURE 9-1   (continued)

Criteria	Weight	Maple Road	Civic Center	Downtown	Existing
Legal Matters	7	17	14	17	13
Ownership/Availability	4	2	2	2	1
Easements and Restrictions	2	3	2	3	3
Zoning Regulations	1	3	2	3	3
Utilities Availability	18	54	54	54	54
Water	3	3	3	3	3
Sewer	3	3	3	3	3
Storm	3	3	3	3	3
Power	3	3	3	3	3
Phone	3	3	3	3	3
Gas	3	3	3	3	3
Total Score Scoring: 0 (Worse)-3 (Better)		286	284	300	246

Together, this evaluation team can ask the following questions:

Does the site provide enough space to support the building, parking, and future expansion? In urban areas, library sites tend to be more compact with less green space, while suburban library settings need more parking and tend to provide more space for landscaping so they fit into the surrounding residential area.

Is the shape of the site conducive to construction of an efficient and attractive library? Do site conditions dictate how the library should be situated on the premises? Is this situation most advantageous for visibility and access?

Will the site provide desirable views from inside the building? This will determine whether the library will have many windows and where those windows might be. For example, southern and western exposures will raise heating and air-conditioning costs. Additional window coatings or coverings may be required to protect the print collection from prolonged or excessive sunlight exposure.

Will the site be expensive to develop? Are major utilities available? Are area roads large enough to support library traffic or will the library be responsible for road improvements?

Are soil conditions suitable for building or will extensive and expensive soil replacement be required?

Are there environmental conditions that would increase the cost or compromise the full use of a site? Former industrial use of the site might add toxic cleanup costs to the site development. Wetlands may add great views, but construction setbacks around wetlands will limit the amount of the site available for library use and construction activity.

Once the library board has conducted a site evaluation, it is time to look at total project costs. The library board may have identified the perfect site only to discover that the project exceeds the library's budget (see figure 9-2). By working with the evaluation team, the library board can get realistic estimates on total project costs for sites under consideration and can factor the costs into the final site selection decision.

Although decisions about site selection can be the most controversial part of a library construction project, site evaluation can be conducted in an impartial manner. Facts regarding demographics, traffic patterns, future growth, and site suitability will provide the information the library board will need to reach a decision and present a reasoned case to the community.

FIGURE 9-2   Examples of Project Costs

Site	Building Costs	Site Development Costs	Acquisitions Costs	Total Cost
Maple Road	$7,344,000	$802,932	$500,000	$8,646,932
Civic Center	$7,344,000	$758,123	$224,000	$8,326,123
Downtown	$8,419,000	$327,172	$4,000,000	$12,746,172
Existing	$5,704,000	$69,298	$500,000	$6,273,298

THE BUILDING COMMITTEE

At the point that the entire library board decides to enter into a construction project, a library building committee should be appointed. This committee should be a subset of the library board and should include the library director or a representative from the staff. In larger libraries, a specific staff member may be responsible for the planning and maintenance of library facilities. In smaller libraries, this responsibility typically falls to the library director. The library director is usually the library's representative to the architect and contractor and brings to the project the practical experience of how the library operates. Along with the architect's design and engineering knowledge and the contractor's construction expertise, the librarian's experience completes the balance for an efficient building committee.

Once the site is selected and the building committee is appointed, the library can begin planning for construction. This is the point at which the library building committee or trustees should select an architect who will work with them throughout the construction phase. An architect will help the library building committee define its needs more specifically, manage the overall project, and help the library use its resources wisely.

An architect and a good building inspector will be able to evaluate conditions in existing buildings, such as whether the existing building needs new mechanical systems, a roof, parking lots, and interior or exterior site lighting. These professionals can make a reliable decision about whether the building is structurally sound and suitable for a library. Because libraries require extremely high weight-bearing levels for floors, multiple-storied buildings that were not built specifically with library usage in mind usually require additional support. After a thorough inspection, it may be wiser to raze the building and design a building that specifically meets the library's needs.

THE ARCHITECT

The American Institute of Architects (AIA) can assist a building committee in locating architects who have experience designing and building libraries.[3] The AIA also provides materials that help the library building committee evaluate and select the architect best suited to the library's particular situation. The library, the architect, and, eventually, the contractor are the team that will bring the new library to fruition. It is essential that all parties of this team are comfortable working together. Good communication among them will result in a better library building.

Before the architect designs the library, there must be a formal *building program statement*. The building program statement becomes the recipe that will be used to design the building. The program statement describes in detail the types and sizes of spaces the library requires in order to operate efficiently and effectively.

The responsibility of writing the statement may be delegated to the library director and staff depending on the amount of time available and the library director's experience. The architect may assist the staff through the process. However, in most cases, the library board is apt to hire a library consultant to work with the library director and staff to prepare the statement. The consultant that assisted in the needs assessment might be a logical and cost-effective choice as that person is already familiar with the community demographics and library needs.

The building committee and architect may decide to visit other local libraries or notable library buildings around the country. Library directors are usually pleased to show off their new facilities and to point out the strengths and weaknesses of the finished product. A fledgling building committee finds it is easy to learn from the mistakes of others. By visiting other libraries, the building committee and architect can talk about the tone, style, finishes, spaces, and services that will best suit the library project. The tours help the library building committee determine what is needed and desired for the new library.

Before the actual design of the building begins, the library staff and architect must discuss adjacencies in the proposed building. *Adjacencies* define how the various areas of the library will relate to each other. Adjacencies will determine

> which library service areas need to be near the front door, loading dock, or staff entrance,
>
> which departments should be next to each other, and
>
> which departments must be on the first floor or could be in a basement or on a second floor.

Based on this discussion, the architect will divide the building project into four parts: schematics, design development, construction drawings, and construction.[4] *Schematic design* focuses on the adjacencies that have been established. The architect will develop a preliminary building design based on the established adjacencies and the service area sizes as stated in the building program statement. The schematic plan will resemble a series of bubbles sized according to the building program statement and clustered in accordance with the agreed-upon adjacencies. In the *design development* phase, the schematics are refined so that the shape and size of each service area are given more detail. At this point a recognizable floor plan will emerge from the schematic drawings. It is common for construction estimates to be done at the end of design development to make sure the project is within the established budget. It is easier and more cost-effective to add or subtract features from the project at this point. *Construction drawings,* which take considerably longer than schematics and design development, provide the true blueprint of the building. The construction drawings will detail the size of each door and wall and the placement of electrical and data outlets. The construction drawings will provide all the information the contractor needs to bid on and later build the building.

Any change proposed after the completion of the construction drawings will be reflected in a *change order.* Change orders can be initiated by the owner based on a change in finishes or room details or a change in the building program statement. The architect and contractor may initiate change orders based on errors in the blueprints, on-site conditions, or more cost-effective ways to construct the library building. Change orders are expected and budgeted for in any project, but they can be costly and can cause delays in the construction. The more detail there is in the construction drawings, the less likely there will be change orders.

THE CONTRACTOR

Once the construction drawings are complete, the project can go out to bid. This is where the third team member is selected—the contractor. The architect will advertise that the library is seeking a contractor to construct the library based on the construction drawings. After reviewing the construction drawings for several weeks, contractors will bid on the project. The bid will reflect the cost of all building materials, labor, and supervision necessary to construct the library building.

The library typically has two choices of construction supervision to consider—a construction manager or a general contractor. Depending on the library's needs, interests, and abilities, using a construction manager may or may not be appropriate. A *construction manager* is used in projects that are difficult because of historic renovations, in projects with difficult scheduling, or in projects that are very large. Projects using construction managers may be bid out in pieces so the project can get off to an early start. A construction manager may recommend different ways of actually constructing the building that will save the project time and money. Recommendations may include the use of different construction materials, different sequencing of the construction, or a different construction process that might be more efficient. Construction managers work for the owner or the library and should keep the library and architect informed and involved at all stages of the project. Construction management requires more involvement in the construction process on the library's part and will consume more time on the part of the library director or building committee.

General contractors work more independently than construction managers. The library hires a general contractor to articulate the architect's blueprints. The general contractor assumes the decision-making responsibility and does not consult the library or architect on individual decisions. This allows the library director or building committee to be detached from the daily details of construction. If conflicts between the owner and general contractor arise, the architect may offer an impartial opinion, but the general contractor actually supervises the project while the architect only observes.

Regardless of the style of construction management used, good communication between the project team of the library, architect, and contractor is essential. The architect offers the design and structural experience, the contractor provides the construction experience, and the library representative offers the functional experience. Challenges will arise in any project, and only through involvement of all three can the best solutions be found.

CONCLUSION

A library construction project planned by a building committee that works with good consultants, architects, and contractors can run smoothly and successfully. A thoughtful needs assessment, careful site selection, and a detailed building program statement provide the architect the information necessary to design a building that will meet community needs and expectations. The architect who carefully listens to the needs expressed by the building committee and staff will design a building that better meets the library board's expectations. The contractor who is diligent in following the architect's blueprint, is willing to suggest improvements to the proposed plan, and adheres to the project budget and schedule is more likely to build a library building that will satisfy all parties.

The key to the entire library construction project's success will be good communication among all the members of the project team. The dream of the perfect library consisting of books, bodies, and buildings comes true through good communication, unending patience, and a well-coordinated project team.

NOTES

1. Lee B. Brawner, *Determining Your Public Library's Future Size: A Needs Assessment and Planning Model* (Chicago: ALA, 1996), x.
2. Christine Koontz, *Library Facility Siting and Location Handbook* (Westport, Conn.: Greenwood Press, 1997), 85–108.
3. AIA Access: AIA Consumer Site, 2002. Available at http://www.aia.org/consumer. Accessed 17 November 2002.
4. Richard C. McCarthy, *Designing Better Libraries* (Fort Atkinson, Wis.: Highsmith, 1995), 41–77.

10

Furnishing and Equipping a Public Library

While the library board is making arrangements to lease, remodel, or build a facility, planning should be under way for furnishing and equipping the library for public and staff use. Good space planning is essential in making any building functional and attractive. An architect or interior designer will lay out the library interior, but it is essential that staff provide input to the planning. Staff members will know what kinds of services will be offered and the types of equipment they will need to provide those services and should convey those needs to the architect. Visits to other libraries will help the staff, library board, and space planner see how different libraries address different service areas and will help the staff and board articulate space needs to the space planner.

Interior design involves far more than finish, color, or fabric selection for furniture and fixtures. It involves a space needs analysis and careful consideration of traffic flow within the building to determine where people will congregate, where equipment will be placed, and where the best locations are for service desks so staff can supervise the public areas of the building. Careful planning considers how each function (checkout, reference, programming, staff work areas) can be laid out within the space allowed in a way that permits the staff and public to work, study, or conduct research. How can the library planners maximize the use of space while providing an atmosphere that is welcoming and easy to maintain? Does the community architectural style dictate the type of furniture that the library should have? Should it be ultramodern or warm and cozy? What kind of floor, service desk, and wall finishes will provide the durability needed for a public library space while contributing to the ambience of the space? To a certain extent, these are matters of personal taste; however, a professional interior designer will be able to lead the library decision makers through the process by pointing out the advantages and disadvantages of each choice.

Another attribute the interior designer brings to a building project is expertise in selecting appropriate furniture. Unlike purchases made for a private home, furniture and equipment purchased for a public library are expected to last decades. Typically, furnishing a library is underwritten by special funding that may not be available again until an addition or a major renovation is done on the original building, so purchasing furniture that will hold up after years of use is important. Public use of furniture and equipment is far different from use in a private home. Not only are users less careful when using public furniture than they would be when using their home furniture, but also the volume of use is exponentially higher than that which would occur in a private home. This public use and abuse must be considered when selecting finishes and furniture. In her book *Selecting Library Furniture,* Carol Brown goes into great detail on chair and table construction.[1] She discusses the various kinds of joints, edges, and construction techniques that go into the making of good library furniture. Her detailed analysis is helpful when selecting furniture for a public library.

An interior designer can prepare specifications for furniture size and construction, advertise for and review bids from suppliers, place orders, and supervise the installation of purchased furniture and equipment. The specifications usually are written to a particular brand of furniture to indicate the level of quality, exact size, or type of style desired. Many pieces of furniture can look alike, but the joint construction and quality of fabrics and finishes may vary greatly and will affect the usable life of the furniture. The library should allow for competitive bidding as long as the product bids meet the specifications given in the bid proposal. Whether the bid package is advertised in local papers or trade journals, or whether it is sent to prequalified manufacturers, it is essential that all bids are reviewed in great detail and that the item bid actually meets the bid specifications. Although low bids are always welcome, poor-quality furniture in a public library is never a good investment.

Bid prices should include delivery and installation. Although installation of seating usually only involves the removal of plastic shipping bags, the installation of tables and shelving can involve far more than "some assembly required." The installation of library furniture may take between two and eight weeks depending upon the size of the project and therefore must be factored into the project schedule and budget.

In tightly budgeted projects, the library might want to consider reusing existing furniture. Reupholstering and refinishing of good institutional furniture can go a long way to stretch a library budget. Existing steel shelving can be cut down, reconfigured, and electrostatically painted. By installing new end panels and tops, old shelving can look like new and provide many extra years of service. The decision to reuse shelving should be weighed against the cost of dismantling, moving, storing, refinishing, and reinstalling.

SERVICE DESK FUNCTIONS

To better serve the customers, public libraries are generally divided by functions that are identified by service desks. As customers enter the library, staff at an information desk should welcome them and offer any directional assistance needed to rest rooms, water fountains, major service areas, copiers, and so on. In smaller libraries, staff members at the check-in and checkout desk often handle this function; however, in larger buildings, it is better to separate the directional assistance from check-in and checkout activities, even if the same group of employees staffs the desks.

One of the largest pieces of furniture in a library is the check-in and checkout desk. The library check-in and checkout desk has changed a great deal over the years. Initially it might have been the only staffed desk in the library, providing directional advice, library card registration, and check-in and checkout of library materials, and providing a place to pick up materials on hold, pay fines, and receive reference service. To best serve this diverse range of services and to provide supervision of the general library, the desk was typically situated at the main entrance of the building. In small libraries today, this single service point may still be functional, but more often than not even small libraries have established separate service desks for staff serving children, adults, or seniors.

Usually the first function to be moved from this single service desk is the reference service. Larger libraries will provide separate service desks for directional services, children's services, and adult services. Each of these services requires a desk with specialized characteristics of storage, height, access, and possibly shape.

If the library maintains a traditional service of checking materials in and out for the public, the circulation desk should include several staff workstations to accommodate busy times. The equipment should be easily accessible to the staff and somewhat screened from the public. There is, however, a growing trend toward self-service in libraries, especially for checking materials in and out and for picking up materials on hold. New equipment allows customers to have library cards authenticated, retrieve reserved materials from the holds shelf, check out materials, and have the security feature activated, all without staff intervention. Libraries adopting this self-service model of operation can reduce the number of staff needed to facilitate checkout. The information desk in many libraries is evolving into a customer service desk, handling library card registration, fine collection, and directional service. Returned materials are placed in a return slot that allows staff to handle the task of checking in library materials in a nonpublic area and at times that are convenient for the library schedule.

SERVICE DESK DESIGN

Whether the library is using the more traditional circulation desk or a self-service model, a fair amount of equipment, such as security gates, resensitizing equipment for the library's book theft protection system, computers for material checkout, public phones, photocopiers, staff phones, cash registers, and book trucks, is necessary in the circulation desk area. All of this activity and equipment must be considered when selecting a service desk design and layout.

Many libraries opt for a service desk ordered from a library supplier (e.g., Gaylord, Demco, Highsmith). These companies offer modular desks that can be reconfigured, added to, and moved easily. Desktop surfaces of laminate, wood, linoleum, granite, or other solid surface material can be specified from the furniture vendor. Each of these surface materials has cost and durability consequences in addition to aesthetic characteristics. The desktop can be confined to each module, thus allowing for any changes in the configuration that might be needed later. The top can be one continuous surface, which limits the reconfiguration options. This design does offer a more finished look and permits easy sliding of materials to and from customers or between staff workstations without the impediment of seams or openings.

A second option is to have the desk custom designed. The interior designer will discuss the specific functions of the desk with the staff and then design it to meet local needs. The designer will provide shop drawings, which must be carefully reviewed by the staff before the desk goes out to bid. The desk construction can be bid out with other millwork in the library and can incorporate some of the building's design features, such as a trim or window pattern that may be seen throughout the building or a color or material type common to the building. Costs and quality between the two options may not vary, so the decision to use standard modules or to design and build from scratch should be a local decision based on budget and design intent.

Regardless of the desk source, it will be one of the most frequently used pieces of furniture in the library. Millions of items will be dragged across the top surface. Customers will rest their tote bags, purses, and children on the desk edge while they conduct business with the staff. The desk will be in use every hour that the library is open and, if designed well, can make a good impression on the customer and provide highly functional service for the staff.

Features to be considered in designing the desk include:

Desk height. Will staff provide service while standing or sitting? The Americans with Disabilities Act (ADA) requires that individuals using wheelchairs can comfortably use the desk from either the public side or the staff side. Will the desktop surface be a continuous height or step down for special service?

Shape. Will the desk be straight, saw-toothed, or curved? Is a toe space provided on both sides of the desk to prevent people from kicking the desk as they approach it?

Equipment placement. How many computers and staff workstations will be needed at the desk? Will a cash register be on or near the desk? Will equipment be recessed into the work surface or placed on top of the desk? Where will the staff phone be placed? Placement of equipment off the desktop or recessed into the desk provides a cleaner, neater, more welcoming appearance.

Wiring. Will electrical current be in the floor, in the walls, or built into the desk? Will the wiring be out of sight, but still accessible to staff as equipment will be moved and replaced? Will the computer connections and wires be shielded from public view and out of reach of inquisitive fingers?

Placement. Can the staff see library entrances and exits to supervise them easily? Can directions to the rest rooms, pay phones, photocopiers, and other service areas be conveniently given from the desk location? Can the staff leave the desk area to assist the public? The placement of the desk in relation to building columns will impact staff visibility to the public and can hinder giving directions to other areas of the library. Is there space in front of the desk for the public to line up during busy times? It is essential that lines do not block library ingress and egress.

Self-checkout. If customers are checking out their own materials, will the desk accommodate sufficient self-check stations? Can the staff monitor the use of the equipment in order to offer customer assistance when necessary?

Applications and standard forms. Will customers be offered space to fill out library application forms at the desk or will they be asked to fill out forms somewhere else? Will suggestion forms or library promotional pamphlets be available at the desk? Where else might they be distributed or stored? Planning for adequate storage will allow the staff to provide service without leaving the desk to retrieve forms.

Lost and found. Will lost and found items be stored in or at the desk? Is there a locked place for lost valuables?

Library materials. Will items being held for customers be kept at the desk or somewhere else in the library? Where will library materials be returned? Where will library materials be sorted? Where will book carts or trucks to reshelve materials be stored?

Flooring. Will special flooring be provided on the staff side of the desk for staff members who stand most of the day or evening? Will the floor material add noise to the area when book trucks are rolled across it?

The checkout desk is not the only public service desk in many medium-sized or large libraries. Separate service desks may be maintained for children's, teen, adult, or senior citizen services so the desks can be closer to the collections the staff needs to access. The library may have a separate service area for audiovisual, periodical, or popular materials. In larger libraries, each area should have its own service desk designed to serve that specific clientele. In order to provide eye-to-eye service, the children's desk should be about thirty inches high. Librarians at adult services desks sometimes prefer the thirty-nine-inch-high desk in order to allow staff to make eye-to-eye contact with library customers while staff members are seated.

Each service desk could have a different configuration depending on where it is situated in its service area and the type of equipment. Most service desks have at least one computer and one printer that provide access to the Internet and library holdings. All service desks typically have at least one telephone and may have four or five depending on the number of staff stationed at the desk. Reference desks typically have fax and photocopy machines close by. It is not uncommon for reference desks to have a seating area where lengthy reference interviews can be conducted or where customers can sit down while being served. Each desk within a library will be different, and the staff working at that desk should be consulted on the desk design and equipment required.

READING CHAIRS

The library should offer the public a variety of seating and study space options, such as quiet study, private study (individual study rooms), semiprivate study (carrels), group study rooms, and large study tables throughout the library. It is important to provide seating for a variety of users. Some library users like absolute quiet, while others enjoy having background noise. Some library users prefer privacy, while others like to see who is coming and going. People using investment and stock market materials might prefer larger tables to spread out their newspapers and research materials. Tutors need private space to work with students, and groups will want to hold their discussions somewhere that does not disturb other library users. Each kind of space can be accommodated within a library plan and furnished in a way that makes the space more usable.

Each library activity will have specific seating needs. Many table manufacturers make table and chair sets, but there are also manufacturers who specialize in chairs only. Because reading chairs are one of the most abused pieces of furniture in a library, it is wise to thoroughly investigate how the chair is made and to look for quality construction. Are the joints constructed to take a lot of stress? Stress is placed on chair joints when chairs are dragged around the library. In addition, when people tip the chair back on the chair's rear legs, joints between the legs and chair seats receive an enormous amount of stress. Sled-base chairs (see figure 10-1) make it more difficult for customers to tip the chair backward. Sled-base chairs also are easier to slide under a table.

Some manufacturers offer two-position chairs, often referred to as "rocker chairs" (see figure 10-2). These chairs combine the easy slide of a sled-base with a tipped back position, allowing the sitter to lean back without the risk of falling or damaging the chair.

Damage is a given even with the best-constructed furniture. People put their feet up on chairs, dirtying fabric and scratching wood seats. If chair arms hit the undersides of tables, the chair arms get scratched. When selecting furniture, libraries need to consider how the furniture will be used and abused.

FIGURE 10-1   Worden
sled-base chair

FIGURE 10-2   Worden rocker-base
chair

Another seating option to consider is stools. Library users enjoy sitting on short stools while browsing materials in the stacks, especially if those resources are on lower shelves. Lightweight stools can be moved easily by adults and children and placed where the user needs the seat. Most libraries provide step stools in the stacks to allow customers to reach higher shelves, and it is not uncommon to see a customer sitting on a step stool. A nicer solution is for the library to provide separate lower, rolling step stools and higher, stool-type seating for browsing purposes.

STUDY TABLES

Library study tables will be heavily used by the public and lifted and moved by cleaning staff and therefore should be carefully evaluated for stability, sturdiness, and weight. Table weight can stress table joints, so solid construction is important. Performance testing on tables evaluates a table's vertical load capacity, its resistance to deflection (stiffness), and its resistance to sideways and front-to-back loads. The style of construction and the material the table is made of both contribute to the durability and life expectancy of the table.

Tables should be selected to meet the needs of customers and staff in the specific areas in which the tables will be used. The needs of people with disabilities and compliance with ADA also should be considered in each of the library's service areas. At least one study table that can accommodate a person in a wheelchair should be available in each area of the library. Particular attention should be paid to the aprons that are usually found under a table edge. The apron can cut an inch or two of height off the accessible area under the table, making it impossible to slide a wheelchair underneath the table.

Another special need area is the children's room. The children's room is an active area in any public library and, in addition to being sturdy, the furniture must be kid-proof—that is, without sharp edges or corners and with shapes and colors that appeal to young children. Although designed for children, furniture in the children's part of the library will also be used by adults, so the chairs must be able to support an adult's weight. The ideal table height for young children is between twenty and twenty-two inches. Because these tables are short, adults often sit on them, so the tables need to bear that weight without breaking.

The work and seating surface on children's tables and chairs should be easy to clean. Accidents with craft materials and bodily functions are not uncommon in a children's library. Style does not have to be sacrificed for durability, as hundreds of laminates are available to perk up the look of furniture in the children's services area. With the use of colorful carpeting, upholstery, and wall colors and coverings as well as attractive shelving and end panels, a children's room can be practical as well as appealing to all visitors.

Furniture needs to be progressively sized to suit preschoolers through preteens. Older children need bigger furniture than that found in the preschoolers' area. Children in elementary school are comfortable at tables that are between twenty-four and twenty-six inches high with chair seats between fifteen and sixteen inches high. A parent helping his or her child with homework can also comfortably use twenty-four-inch-high tables. Round tables are popular for group work and again provide an edge that is safe for children of all ages.

For teens and adults the tabletops should be at least twenty-nine inches high. Unlike children, teenagers and adults tend to spread their research materials out and require more personal space. If the tabletop is less than seventy-two inches wide, it is unlikely that two strangers will use the table at the same time. A seventy-two-by-thirty-inch table will provide enough space for two adults to sit at opposite corners of the table and work.

Teenagers, on the other hand, will squeeze as many chairs around a table as possible. Teens tend to visit libraries in groups, and providing a separate space for them to talk and study both attracts them and isolates their noise and activity from quieter areas of the library. Libraries that plan to limit table seating to four people at a table might want to consider tables with full-panel or plank stretchers on the ends. This makes it difficult for people to pull up additional chairs at table ends. When table seating is limited to four people, it is easier to control noise and rowdiness. Library books, DVDs, CDs, and magazines specifically selected for teens can be gathered together in an area of the library that is designed for teens.

Height and table size are only two of the issues to consider when selecting tables. Another option libraries should consider is to wire study tables for computer usage. Most furniture manufacturers offer wire management systems that bring power and data connections to the tabletop. Some of these tables are rated by Underwriters Laboratories (UL) and are marked with the ⓊⓁ mark. The UL mark on a product means that UL has tested and evaluated representative samples of that product and determined that they meet UL's requirements for safety.[2] In effect, the table becomes an appliance that allows users to plug in personal computers or other electrical equipment for access to electricity or the library's data network.

More and more libraries rely upon wireless technology for data transmission. Because laptop computer batteries only last a few hours, having an electrical outlet at workstations is a boon to library users. If the library chooses not to bring power to the table, some tables should be within easy reach of wall outlets to accommodate laptop computer users.

CASUAL SEATING

Not everyone coming to the library wants to sit at a table to read or study. Parents and grandparents like to cuddle up with their children and grandchildren to read stories, so they prefer love seats or large chairs for this activity. Whether the library supplies a large rocker or an upholstered sofa, all the furniture should be inviting and comfortable for adults and young children alike.

Teens like furniture that is trendy, interesting, and colorful. Designers have a lot of fun designing teen areas, and many libraries have found it helpful to consult with teen advisory groups when selecting furniture for areas that primarily serve that special population. Furniture that works in a teen's home may not withstand the heavy use such furniture will get in a public library. That is why commercial-grade furniture is available in bold colors and patterns that appeal to teens. On the other hand, the library may opt for less-durable and trendier furniture for a teen area and replace that furniture more frequently.

Just as young children and teens have unique seating needs, adults have seating preferences. Some adults enjoy library lounge furniture for reading magazines, newspapers, or books. On occasion, adults might share a sofa, but generally speaking, single seats will be more popular. End tables and lamps will add ambiance to a reading room and make this space feel more like a private library or living room. If the furniture is arranged around an area rug, a fireplace, or a patio or tucked into an alcove, readers will enjoy a sense of privacy and quiet comfort. These reading areas should be removed from high-traffic areas to create a peaceful and relaxing reading retreat.

Furniture construction materials should be consistent with the mission and purpose of the library or service area. Libraries with a more traditional look might use wood furniture. Libraries that want a contemporary look might use metal finishes. But whether the library desires a traditional or contemporary feel, the texture, color, and pattern of fabric can be dramatic. The furniture can complement or create a contrast to other finishes in a room with subtle floor coverings and bold-colored and -patterned furniture. Upholstered furniture can create comfortable spaces that many people expect to find in their public library. However, fabric can generate high maintenance costs if it is not carefully selected. How does one know if a fabric will survive the hard use it will get? Fabric manufacturers give wearability codes to their fabrics. The rating is measured in "double rubs," or the number of times a piece of fabric can be rubbed back and forth before showing wear. The key to selecting fabric for public seating is to make sure it has a high double rub rating. Because public libraries keep furniture a very long time and furniture in public spaces gets such heavy use, drapery fabrics or residential upholstery fabric should not be used for seating. Only fabric exceeding 25,000 double rubs should be considered for library office furniture, and only fabrics in the 50,000 double rub or higher ranges should be considered for public areas of the library. Prints are generally preferable over solids, as they don't show dirt or wear as easily. Regular cleaning of upholstery extends fabric life, as ground-in dirt is hard on fabric. With careful selection and maintenance, a library's upholstered furniture can offer years and sometimes decades of service.

Leather might be a consideration for some library seating. Although it will cost more, commercial-grade leather is durable in a public building. Consider such characteristics as light fastness, aniline dyes, and abrasion tolerances when selecting leather.

Whether using fabric or leather, it is not wise to upholster the arms of chairs, because this area is typically the first to show wear. A wood or metal cap on the arm will avoid excessive wear in that area and will extend the life of the chair upholstery for years.

SPECIAL USE FURNITURE AND EQUIPMENT

Certain pieces of equipment require specialized furniture. For instance, computers that will be used for any length of time should be on tables that provide enough work space (a minimum of forty-eight inches per person) to accommodate library materials and the computer. Computers are getting smaller and more compact, especially those with flat screens, so the depth of the table is not as crucial as the width. Be sure to measure the depth of the keyboard and monitor to make sure they both fit on the table. Libraries providing individual printers for each computer must provide larger work surfaces to accommodate the printer. To save space, the library should consider networked printing. Networked printers cut down on the number of printers that need to be maintained as well as the size of the work surface needed at each workstation. By combining networked printers with debit card machines, the library can recoup some of the printing costs.

With the amount of time that people spend in front of computers today, ergonomics has become more important. Each user should be able to easily adjust the chairs at computer workstations. The adjustments on the chairs should be easy for the user to understand and manipulate. Articulating keyboards are a way to improve ergonomics, but with adjustable chairs, the need for the articulating keyboard is lessened. Some people find the articulating keyboard awkward to use, and other people just can't find them.

In past years, there was interest in mounting computer monitors under the work surface with viewing occurring through a glass panel in the tabletop. There are advantages and disadvantages to these tables. The advantages are that undermounted monitors provide a little more privacy and keep more of the tabletop clear. However, the disadvantages are that the glass panels can get scratched when books are dragged across the glass and the monitor consumes space under the tabletop and compromises leg room. After long periods of use, some people complain of neck strain from having to look down at the computer screen, and glare can be an issue. To combat the glare, libraries have placed plastic shields at the top of the glass opening, thus compromising the amount of work surface available. With the advent of flat screens, there is less need to consider the undermounted monitors.

Although more and more information is being provided via the Internet, there is still a need for microfilm and microfiche readers and printers, closed-circuit TV, and scanning equipment for the visually impaired. These machines tend to be large and require a deep table as well as a wide work area for note taking next to the machine. Some tables even allow the user to adjust the work surface height to improve viewing.

Study carrels are popular in many libraries and can be designed for one, two, or four users. The single-person carrels provide a bit more privacy than the multiple-seat carrels and a lot more flexibility for the library. The four-person carrel becomes quite large and is less inviting than the single-person carrel. The carrels also come with different-height sides. The panel facing the user should be at least above eye level. If full side panels are used, a light should be provided under the shelf. However, side panels need not be high, nor do they need to reach all the way to the front of the tabletop. Carrels with the lower side profiles provide more light without sacrificing privacy. It is also nice to provide a shelf in the carrel so the user can stack research material, leaving the work surface more open.

Public meeting rooms also have specialized furniture needs. Some libraries may have an angled floor with fold-down fixed seating, similar to theater seating, facing a stage. The room may be equipped for video- or teleconferencing. It may even have professional stage lighting and theater curtains. However, most libraries have flat-floored meeting rooms that allow for chairs to be configured as needed, with or without tables. Stacking chairs generally are metal framed with either a plastic or an upholstered seat. The upholstered seats can be damaged when stacking the chairs. And although plastic seats tend to be more durable, they don't breathe like an upholstered seat and are thus slightly less comfortable for people to sit on during longer meetings or programs. Also, many of the chairs have some built-in flexibility in the backs that makes them more comfortable than chairs with fixed backs. The feature of flexibility is definitely a worthwhile investment. Sometimes the chairs can lock to each other to form a straight row, or they may remain totally independent of the chair next to them. Rolling caddies used to stack and store the chairs are also essential purchases.

Meeting room tables should be easy to move. Both the public and staff will reconfigure the room on a regular basis, so it is worthwhile investing in lightweight rolling and folding tables. *Lightweight* is a relative word, because typical sixty-by-thirty-inch tables can weigh over ninety pounds, while the lightweight model in the same size might weigh about sixty-five pounds. Even more convenient are the lightweight sixty-by-eighteen-inch tables that weigh a mere forty-eight pounds. A lightweight sixty-by-eighteen-inch table with casters and wheel locks provides a flexible option that just about anyone can configure. As with the stacking chairs, it is helpful to order caddies to more easily move the tables around the room.

Because libraries use a lot of audiovisual materials for programming, the meeting room should be equipped with a large screen, preferably motorized, that can be viewed from anywhere in the room. Another choice might be the use of a white-board wall, which can serve as a projection screen, marker board, or magnetic board. White-board walls are not merely painted walls, but are metal panels affixed to walls that allow presenters to use dry markers and magnets. Ideally, a library would provide both a projection screen and white board because the projection screen presents a better image with no glare for audience viewing. In a pinch, however, the white board can serve double duty. Room-darkening shades will also facilitate a better image on the screen or wall.

Other amenities that might be considered to protect meeting room walls would be tackable surfaces and picture rails. Speakers often want to display posters or other graphics with tape or tacks, causing possible damage to meeting room walls and wall coverings. Tackable surfaces prevent this damage. A picture rail is a piece of molding mounted near the ceiling from which presenters can hang pictures suspended by wire. A picture rail protects walls from nail holes and allows for changing pictures and displays with ease. Another benefit is that when not in use, the picture rail is unobtrusive.

There are many other specialized pieces of equipment that libraries may want to consider including display cases, pamphlet racks, public bulletin boards, change machines, and public fax machines. Each library will have to determine the appropriate mix of furniture and equipment that will enhance service without compromising collection storage, general ambience, or budgets. Regardless of library size, designers must consider comfort, style, and durability when selecting furniture and fixtures.

SHELVING

The core of any library is its collection of materials. In the past, libraries consisted primarily of books, and shelving books was fairly easily managed. Printed materials still make up the largest portion of most public library collections, but nonprint materials (CDs, DVDs, videos, cassette tapes, puppets, etc.) have become some of the most popular and well-used collections in public libraries. These new information formats offer some shelving challenges while at the same time offering great marketing and display opportunities. Having the right shelving for each item will help staff members keep the library attractive and usable.

Selecting the right shelving for each application can be daunting, and it is best to work with either the manufacturer's representative or an experienced library planner when selecting shelving. Just as important as the selection is proper installation of shelving. Some areas of the country may require special anchoring or bracing of shelving to prevent collapse in the event of an earthquake. It is also necessary to begin this process of identifying shelving needs early in your facility planning as shelving often has a long lead time, even when you are ordering standard colors and items.

Whether selecting all wood shelving or steel shelving, library designers are wise to investigate the shelving's stability, strength, and ease of adjustment. Wood shelving is one of the hallmarks of older libraries, but it can be very costly. Steel shelving can provide a practical, safe, and attractive alternative to wood. Wood end panels and steel shelving can provide the warmth of wood in a room without the added expense of all wood shelving. An even more economical approach is to use steel shelving with steel end panels that can be commercially painted to match any decor.

If wood shelving is selected, it is important that the shelves are easily adjustable. As proof of this need, books in the library's art section are significantly taller and wider than the typical novel. It is not uncommon to see books shelved on their sides to accommodate an occasional large tome. If most of the books on a shelf are tipped, it is difficult to read spine labels or to find a specific book. The library may consider folio shelves, which are deeper, for special collections like atlases or art books.

The quality of the wood is also important. Books are very heavy, and shelves made of particleboard will tend to sag when fully loaded.[3] Solid wood should be used on all shelf and end panel edges. Careless use of book trucks and cleaning equipment damages end panels, and solid wood edges extend the attractive life of the shelving.

Steel shelving is more common than wood shelving in public libraries because of its lower cost and durability. Steel shelving is also available in a wide variety of colors. It is recommended that libraries use lighter colors for the shelves, which are less likely to show dust and allow the eye to focus on the book and not on the color of the shelf. Custom colors are available and may not initially cost any more than the standard colors offered by shelving manufacturers, but if the library wants to expand its shelving later on, the upcharge for a custom color can be prohibitive.

It is essential that a reputable library shelving manufacturer be used to ensure that the finish is smooth, the paint won't chip, and the steel is heavy gauge. Library steel shelving is designed with the strength necessary to hold library book collections as well as the ability to adjust shelf heights easily and to add on to existing shelving at a later date. The shelving should have a base shelf, end panel, and canopy to create a finished look.

Another feature worth considering in shelving design is the integrated back. This extra bend in the metal adds extra strength to the shelf and prohibits materials from slipping back beyond the shelf into the shelves on the other side of the unit. The disadvantage of the integrated back is that it does not allow larger materials to be pushed farther back on the shelf to create a smooth front edge to the collection. However, when large items are shelved with book spines flush with the front of the shelf, materials on shelves behind can be pushed out or displaced. The integrated back also offers the library the opportunity to connect bookends to the shelf at the lower back edge, rather than hanging them from above or having them completely detached from the shelving unit.

Choosing between wood or steel shelving is only one decision that needs to be made. Shelving depth is another issue to consider as shelving depth needs will change in different parts of the library. Library shelving manufacturers offer standard shelves in eight-, ten-, and twelve-inch depths. Although these are the depths given, in fact the shelves are only usable for seven, nine, or eleven inches, respectively. Most general shelving needs can be met with the ten-inch shelf. The twelve-inch shelf is good for reference materials and picture books, but is too deep for fiction and nonfiction. If a deeper shelf than is necessary is used, the materials tend to drift toward the back of the shelf, leaving the front edge of book spines ragged and not flush with the front of the shelf.

Today, there are many specialty shelves available to libraries. Some of the common types include divided shelves, CD drawers, media shelves, kick-out shelving, hinged periodical shelving, pullout reference shelves, and compact shelving. Divided shelves are particularly popular in the children's picture or easy book areas. The thin metal dividers are placed three to five per shelf and help keep the books upright. Some libraries are using divided shelving throughout the library as it lessens the need for traditional book supports. CD drawers allow libraries to shelve CDs and DVDs face out, as is commonly seen in music stores. The drawers are amazingly compact and can be very helpful in marketing library materials. Media shelves with tipped bottoms help showcase the material. Kick-out shelving takes the tipping of shelves even farther. When the bottom three shelves of the shelving unit are angled out, it becomes very easy to browse lower shelves. Periodicals can be stored either on fixed shelves that allow libraries to display a single issue or on hinged shelving that allows for some storage of back issues behind the shelf. Pullout reference shelves can be affixed anywhere in the collection and provide a temporary work surface in the stacks. Compact shelving has been used to store less frequently used materials, such as back issues of periodicals. It is available in either an electronic model or a manual crank model and saves a great deal of floor space. Because it eliminates aisles, compact shelving requires special floor supports. When fully loaded, it will increase the weight placed on the floor. Floors designed for regular shelving must be able to support 150 pounds per square foot, whereas floors designed to support compact shelving must support 300 pounds per square foot. A three-foot, double-faced unit of shelving can weigh over a ton, so it is essential that architects design floors that can bear that weight. The options in terms of style, color, accessories, and sizes in shelving ensure that there will be shelving to meet every need in every library.

Shelving is also available in just about any height a library would need. The most popular standard heights are forty-four, sixty-six, seventy-two, eight-four, and ninety inches high. The lower sections are often used behind a service desk as they provide storage, but do not block views from the service desk. The low level of the shelving makes an ideal work surface as well. Sixty-six-inch-high shelving is most commonly used in the children's section because the shelving is low enough for most children to reach materials on the top shelf. Shelving over seventy-four inches high is used in adult areas. The higher shelving offers more storage, but top shelves may block light in the building and can be difficult for people to reach. If tall shelving blocks general lighting in the area, the library may want to consider purchasing light fixtures that are attached to the shelving itself. This ensures that light is washed over the front of the entire shelving unit, making it easier for customers and staff to read book spines and to find material in the library.

Not only is shelving available in a wide range of heights, but it can be wall hung, single faced, or double faced. Wall-hung shelving can be extremely cost-effective if the library has wall space available on which to mount the shelving brackets. Single-faced shelving has special supports that allow for placing shelving along a wall that may not be able to support wall-hung shelving. The most commonly used shelving consists of double-faced units that allow library materials to be shelved on two sides.

Although it is recommended that shelving be placed in rows that are five feet on center, wider aisles add to the spacious feeling in a library. Different brands of shelving have different footprints. Kick-out shelving can be several inches wider than traditional shelving, and this must be taken into consideration when laying out the shelving in order to maintain a thirty-six-inch-wide clear aisle to comply with ADA standards.

A single row of shelving is called a *range* of shelving, and ranges of shelves that are clustered together by collection are referred to as *stacks*. Stacks will take up a significant amount of space within a library. The space is consumed both vertically and horizontally. There is no getting around the fact that shelving can quickly fill a building. One of the ways to lessen the visual impact of shelving is to provide breaks in the stacks. Ideally, ranges should not exceed twenty-four feet in length without a cross aisle. Stacks can be broken up with a row of study tables or widened to feature a piece of art or a window at the end of the aisle. Creative placement of shelving can enhance the building design, but the sequence of placement must be intuitive. Libraries shelve materials in specific order, so shelving should help lead users through the collection and not confuse them by twisting and turning. Consideration must be given to how the collection can be logically arranged on the floor and how shelving can best facilitate the use of the library's resources.

FURNITURE IN NONPUBLIC AREAS OF THE LIBRARY

Although employees spend a great deal of time in the public areas of the library, it is important that work space for staff be provided in a nonpublic area. Although staff furniture is not used or abused as much as furniture found in the public areas, it is just as important to take time to order the right furniture. Attractive and well-planned work spaces will provide a pleasant environment for everyone. If all new furniture is purchased for public areas and staff areas are not freshened, staff morale may become an issue. People take pride in their work area, and money spent on staff furniture can reap the benefits of a happier staff for the library.

Systems furniture that is used in the setup of floor plans and office space cubicles works well in library staff areas. Systems furniture consists of individual components that allow a great deal of flexibility and can be reconfigured as needed. The modular nature of systems furniture will facilitate creating separate work spaces for individuals or for work groups without erecting permanent walls. By changing materials, colors, or component heights, the library can create individualized, inexpensive work spaces. From the maintenance staff to the director's office, systems furniture can be functional and attractive.

Work surfaces that are large enough to accommodate computers, the processing of library materials, or consultation of multiple resources make for a more productive and pleasant work environment. Employees working with computers will need a minimum of seventy-five square feet of work space per employee. To prevent repetitive stress injuries and fatigue, high-quality adjustable seating is a must for someone who may sit in the same chair all day in front of a computer.

Other important work space considerations include the following:

Electrical, phone, and data outlets should be built into the furniture so people can easily move equipment on their work surface or within their work space.

Good task lighting that is appropriately placed or movable will lessen the risk of eyestrain.

Overhead bins, open shelves, file drawers, box drawers, and tackboards will offer flexible storage for each employee.

Planning of each workstation should involve an analysis of the type of work to be conducted in the space. Designers need to ask such questions as: Does the employee need more work surface and less storage space, or more file space and less countertop? Does the employee sit in one spot all day or does she or he move around within the work space? Does the employee spend all day at that work space or does she or he have a secondary workstation in the public area? All these questions should be considered before selecting staff area furniture. Again, an interior designer or space planner can assist in the selection and specification of individual components of the workstation, and a qualified installer will be needed to assemble the components upon delivery.

FILES

When planning the staff work area, designers cannot overlook the storage of library business materials. The myth of the paperless office becomes more apparent each year. Even with the reliance upon electronic files, the need for paper storage grows daily. Libraries are no different than other office environments that need to store business information. Traditional vertical and lateral file cabinets are still used in many libraries, but larger libraries may want to consider the use of high-density filing systems. These systems may use traditional file cabinets, but stack them front to back and place them on movable tracks. Similar to compact shelving for less frequently used library materials, compact filing cabinets eliminate the aisles between individual cabinets. Another alternative to consider is rack-mounted filing similar to that used for medical records management. Whether open or closed, locked or unlocked, movable or not, file cabinets in the office still seem to be prevalent.

CONCLUSION

Library furniture and equipment are integral components of the library. From large service desks to small reading chairs for toddlers, each piece of furniture will have a range of options and features. A designer can use fabric, color, material, shape, or dimension to craft effective work spaces that are also aesthetically pleasing. Successful projects will include an analysis of the type of work to be accomplished in each area and will include input from the staff working in that area. Manufacturers' representatives, space planners, and interior designers should be consulted for input and direction on maximizing style, comfort, durability, and design while managing the cost of furniture and fixtures.

Take the time to visit other libraries, offices, and manufacturers' showrooms and to visit vendors in the exhibit halls at library conferences. Don't be afraid to ask questions, open drawers, or test furniture. Ask for the opportunity to sit on chairs for several weeks to make sure they will be comfortable and meet the needs of the library. Be leery of trendy furniture, and look for style combined with durability, functionality, easy maintenance, and cost-effectiveness. Decisions made in selecting library furniture and equipment will impact the library for years to come.

Finally, take advantage of advice offered by professional library space planners, interior designers, and manufacturers. These professionals can provide invaluable advice on the strengths and weaknesses of each item. Approach the selection of library furniture and equipment with research, consultation, and testing before you purchase.

NOTES

1. Carol R. Brown, *Selecting Library Furniture: A Guide for Librarians, Designers, and Architects* (Phoenix: Oryx Press, 1989).
2. The UL Mark, 2002. Available at http://www.ul.com/mark. Accessed 17 November 2002.
3. Brown, *Selecting Library Furniture*, p. 22.

11

Developing the Collection

Libraries exist to collect, organize, and provide information to people. Most of this information will come from materials specifically selected and purchased by the library staff to meet the evolving needs of the library's clientele. Today, web resources have become integral parts of a library's collection, and even though these items have not been purchased, librarians evaluate and select specific websites to be included in the library's website or in electronic bookmarks kept at service desks. Librarians refer to this process of acquiring library materials, whether in print or as a link to the library's website, as collection development.

Collection development is the process of selecting materials in all formats to meet a library's needs, goals, objectives, and priorities. It also includes the processes of analyzing these materials to see if they meet the goals and ongoing objectives of the library and then making the materials accessible to the library's users. Collection development policies may also be created to inform the public and staff about the principles upon which selections are made.

The process begins with an approved *collection development plan* that includes

- The library's mission and purpose
- Selection criteria, such as scope, publication date, or price
- Material formats to be collected (print, CD, DVD, video, etc.)
- Responsibility for selection
- Customer requests

- Gifts and donations
- Challenges to library materials
- Weeding

The collection development policy provides an overall view of what the library will be collecting and the extent of the collection. The guidance to acquire, retain, or withdraw specific materials is addressed in the *selection* portion of the collection development policy.

Defining the scope of the library's collection activity helps staff allocate financial resources where they will do the most good. As part of its general policy manual, the library should already have an approved mission that is based on a community profile and the needs of that community. Will the library be a popular materials reading center, or will it provide in-depth reference and research services? Will the library's collections be deeper in certain areas that have particular relevance to the community? For instance, libraries serving non-English-speaking populations may purchase many materials in a language other than English. Will certain collections not be expanded because a neighboring library is focusing heavily in that subject?

Although libraries still purchase many books, audiovisual or nonprint materials have become important parts of the public library collection. Bestsellers may be available in regular-print, large-print, electronic, or audio formats all at the same time. It is not unusual for new books to be published in multiple formats. Library boards need to determine if all *formats* will be acquired and if preference should be given to any format over others.

Depending on state and local laws, *responsibility for selection* of library materials may be restricted to specific individuals in the library. The responsibility may be given to the library director, who will operate in the framework of policies determined by the library board of trustees. In such cases, the director may delegate that responsibility to a staff of librarians with professional education and training in the principles and practices of materials selection.

All librarians have a professional responsibility to be inclusive, not exclusive, in developing collections. Efforts are made to include materials representing all viewpoints on a given subject. Librarians use reviews of new titles published in professionally recognized resources as a primary source for materials selection. Standard bibliographies, book lists by recognized authorities, and the advice of competent people in specific subject areas are also taken into consideration.

Each type of material is considered in terms of its merit and the audience for whom it is intended. No single standard can be applied in all cases. Some materials may be judged primarily in terms of artistic merit, scholarship, or value to humanity; others are selected to satisfy the informational, recreational, or educational interests of the community.

The inclusion of *controversial materials* in the library's collection will undoubtedly lead to critical comments from the public. The library should be prepared to respond to these concerns. This is part of the library profession's commitment to *intellectual freedom,* which is the right of people to seek and receive information on all points of view. If a library staff has done a good job of building a balanced collection, materials will be available on all sides of important controversial issues, such as abortion, evolution, and politics. If the library staff has done a good job of selection, people should agree with only half the material the library owns on any controversial subject. Most libraries adopt the ALA's *Freedom to Read Statement*[1] and the *Library Bill of Rights*.[2] As part of a library's materials selection policy, these two documents support the broad selection of materials and the freedom of people of all ages to read and view those materials. These two documents form the cornerstone of intellectual freedom as articulated in libraries and have direct impact on the selection of materials.

While attempting to build balanced collections, libraries still recognize that the choice of materials for personal use is an individual matter and that the responsibility for the use of materials by children and adolescents rests with their parents or legal guardians. While a person may reject materials for himself or herself or for his or her children, he or she cannot restrict access to the materials by others in a public library. Libraries should have a policy and procedure in place so the community, the board, and the staff know how to address concerns by individuals or groups regarding the inclusion of specific materials in the library's collection. The professional staff and the library board should review any statements of concern submitted to the library, and the customer should be informed of the trustees' decision regarding the challenge. It is helpful to notify the American Library Association's Office of Intellectual Freedom of any such cases. The association is not interested in complainant's names, addresses, or other personal information. ALA is only concerned with tracking the authors, titles, or subjects that are being challenged. Annual statistics compiled on items challenged are helpful in spotting trends.

Although librarians are knowledgeable about the subjects they purchase materials for and rely upon reviews of new titles, *recommendations* of authors, titles, and subjects from members of the general public and other staff should be considered for inclusion in the collection. Considering such recommendations will certainly create goodwill in the community and can greatly enhance the library's collection. Many libraries have organized *tribute and gift programs* that not only welcome suggestions for purchases from the public, but also provide a mechanism by which the money to underwrite those purchases comes to the library. These gift programs provide library supporters a way to recognize special occasions or honor a relative's or friend's birthday, anniversary, or other event. Libraries can also encourage donations and memorials by providing funeral directors with contribution envelopes. Monies received in these allow the library to purchase additional materials in the name of the deceased. Of course, people do not have to give in honor of any special event.

Not all gifts will come in the form of cash donations. Many people want to give libraries used books. Most used books contributed to public libraries end up in library book sales with the profits from those sales coming back to the library for special purchases. The library's collection development policy should address such gifts. Gifts should meet the same selection criteria as purchased materials, and the library should retain unconditional ownership of all donations. The library should also reserve the right to make the final decision on acceptance, use, or disposition of all gift materials.

Some donors may wish to give special collections or memorial collections with a desire to have those materials shelved as separate physical entities. The library should state in its policy whether this will be allowed or whether materials will be integrated into the general collection. Donor recognition should also be a part of the policy. Most libraries insert bookplates in gift books, but other forms of recognition for large contributions might be considered. One form of recognition that should always be given is a letter to the donor for tax purposes, acknowledging the gift. Under IRS guidelines, the appraisal of the gift for tax purposes is the responsibility of the donor, not of the library.

Libraries keep collections vital and useful by retaining or replacing essential materials and by removing, on a systematic and continuous basis, those works that are worn, dirty, outdated, of little historical significance, or no longer in demand. This process is called *weeding the collection* and is just as important as selecting titles to add to the collection. The *CREW* (Continuous Review, Evaluation, and Weeding) manual provides guidelines that many librarians use for collection evaluation and weeding.[3] Once an item has been weeded from the collection, many libraries dispose of the material in their book sales; however, libraries part of larger municipal organizations may have to follow other rules for disposal of public property. Library directors should check with the library's parent body to see if there are restrictions on disposal of public property. Proper weeding improves the entire collection by creating space on shelves for new materials and builds public confidence and interest in the library's collection because customers will know that only current and accurate materials are provided at their public library.

Budgeting for collection development varies from library to library. If the library's goal is the provision of information, then significant amounts of money should be spent on acquiring materials for public use. A general rule is that the library should allocate 20 percent of the annual budget for the purchase of new materials. The library may want to include this goal in the collection development policy and may even want to be more specific and allocate by percentage to specific collections. If the policy gets this detailed, it will have to be frequently reviewed as the library may want to focus collection development in different subject areas each year.

Instead of purchasing new materials (books, CDs, DVDs, videos, and cassettes) directly from publishers or from local retailers, libraries use vendors that can supply materials from a wide variety of publishers. Library vendors like Baker & Taylor, Brodart, and Ingram Library Services also offer libraries significant price discounts on new materials. Discounts are available to individual libraries, but larger discounts are available to library groups. Some library systems negotiate discounts on behalf of their members. Some states have statewide discounts that individual libraries can use. These negotiated agreements might cover a variety of ordering methods, discounts, or free shipping and handling. Libraries will almost always get a better discount if they order under a group plan.

Most libraries do select materials one item at a time, but there are several services offered by library vendors to help in the selection process. Certain books, such as almanacs and travel, medical, and college guides, are usually purchased every year. Magazines and newspapers also are ordered on an annual basis. The librarian can work with the book vendor to identify best-selling authors and automatically have the book vendor ship titles by those authors to the library without the library ordering the titles individually. Book vendors refer to these services as standing orders or continuation services.

Some library vendors also offer assistance with customized collection development programs. These vendors maintain extensive databases of public library–appropriate materials, which they can make available through subscription to local librarians for searching and placing orders. Librarians employed by these vendors can create up-to-date selection lists of titles that local library staffs can use to order materials. Collection development services can include a onetime selection list tailored to a library's specifications,

ongoing monthly lists tailored to a library's specifications, or

customized selection lists with a vendor's professional librarians' purchase recommendations for libraries that do not have the time or staff or both to adequately review a list on their own.

Some libraries use these lists of recommendations to start a new collection for a branch or a bookmobile. The lists can also be used to expand an existing special collection and become an ongoing part of a library's collection development work flow.

Whether the development of the selection list is done by library staff or outsourced to a vendor is a local decision. With a carefully written contract allowing local control and customized selection, a library can use outside vendors for a good portion of the library's technical services work. Improved productivity, a reallocation of limited resources to public service needs, expanded expertise, and potential budget savings can all be achieved by outsourcing technical services. It is important that the library select a vendor that is reliable and experienced so that materials arrive at the library according to the standards established in the contract.

Selecting and ordering the material is only the first step in the acquisitions process. Once the material arrives, it must be cataloged and processed. The cataloging of library materials involves assigning a call number, most often from the Dewey Decimal System, to each book. Libraries can hire technical services personnel to perform these tasks in the library or outsource the work to one of the library vendors. Original cataloging, the process of determining the correct classification number for a particular book, is seldom done in smaller libraries today. Cataloging information becomes a part of the bibliographic record, and these records can be created by the library, acquired from another library's database, purchased along with the material from the vendor, or downloaded from a bibliographic utility that specializes in cataloging, such as OCLC, an international provider of bibliographic records. The electronic bibliographic record, which includes the author, title, publisher, copyright date, classification number, and other identifying information, is needed to create the library's public access catalog (PAC). Specifically designed to receive and display bibliographic records, the PAC is a computerized tool that replaces card catalogs. The PAC allows customers to search the library's holdings by author, title, subject, and format and is the key to accessing the library's collection.

After cataloging, materials need to be processed. This involves applying spine labels, attaching book jackets, and marking the items with the library's name. If the work is outsourced, the material will arrive at the library ready to go on the shelf. The library vendors will tailor the processing to fit the library's specifications so that possession stamps are located in the same spot on all books, spine labels are aligned in accordance with the library's existing collection, and new additions to the library's collection match items already in the collection.

CONCLUSION

Collection development is one of a public library's core tasks. The selection, acquisition, organization, management, and delivery of library materials in a timely manner support other services offered by the library. Customers not finding the titles they want will go elsewhere. Collections filled with outdated books will not be used. Books that are not cataloged correctly will be lost to the staff and public alike. A collection that is not processed with consistent standards will look messy and will be less used than a collection with consistent processing standards. Whether the library does all the work itself or hires a vendor to do the work, consistency in cataloging and processing is essential to maintain the order and uniform appearance of a library's collection. A library's collection is constantly growing and evolving. Librarians need to be diligent in analyzing community interests and needs so that the right material is available at the right time in the right format for each customer.

NOTES

1. *Freedom to Read Statement,* 2000. Available at www.ala.org/alaorg/oif/freeread. html. Accessed 17 November 2002.
2. *Library Bill of Rights,* 1996. Available at www.ala.org/work/freedom/lbr.html. Accessed 17 November 2002.
3. Belinda Boon, *The CREW Method* (Austin: Texas State Library, 1995).

12

Planning and Developing Services

Through the agrarian society, the industrial revolution, and the information age to our 24/7 environment, libraries have endeavored to meet the public's information and entertainment needs. From the funding of the first publicly supported library in 1833 until today, public libraries have adapted, added, and discontinued library services and focus to meet the needs of local communities. The initial focus of public libraries was to loan books. Today, in response to societal interests, the loan service includes a wide range of materials both in print and nonprint formats and in the form of realia, such as puppets and tools.

In the eighteenth and nineteenth centuries, public libraries had little competition from other information providers, but times have changed. The Internet, mega-bookstores, an expanding cable industry, and innumerable pay-for-information services now compete with public libraries. Incorrectly viewed as "free," public libraries are in fact a prepaid service—a service provided by government or association employees and paid for with tax dollars. To remain competitive, libraries have changed the way they do business and the way they look.

Before the end of the nineteenth century, libraries had expanded services beyond the mere loaning of books to the provision of reference service to adults, followed eventually by services to children, young adults, seniors, and people with disabilities. Today's libraries offer "womb to tomb" services. From book bags for newborns to outreach service for the homebound, libraries, based on community analysis and public demand, have customized their service programs to meet the specific needs of a particular community. However, though the delivery mechanisms have changed over time, the core services of lending materials, answering questions, and providing readers' advisory to people of all ages remain an integral part of the library's mission. Later in this chapter, services will be addressed by age groups or by need, but many general services, such as material loans and reference service, are used by all library customers.

MATERIAL LOANS

The most familiar library service is probably that of lending materials, such as books. Librarians refer to the process of loaning materials as "circulation," "charging," or "checkout." Library customers are issued a library card free of charge, although it is not uncommon for libraries to charge a nominal fee for replacing a lost card. Library cards have changed over the years, from small pieces of cardboard with the borrower's name handwritten or typed on them, to plastic cards with bar codes that can be scanned by computers. Now, one is likely to receive a glossy, four-color plastic card embedded with magnetic strips or computer chips. These cards can be used as debit cards to allow customers to use photocopiers or computer printers, to reserve meeting rooms or computers, to download files to a remote server, or to pay fines with money stored, accrued, or debited on the actual card.

Not only do library cards look different than they did years ago, they have different rules for issuance and registration. Some libraries issue a child's library card when the child can write his or her name or when he or she enters school. Some libraries issue different cards to people of different ages. Other libraries will issue a library card at birth, if the parent so requests, with the thought that to delay library card ownership until a certain age or to restrict access to certain collections is age discrimination. A child's card may only provide access to certain collections, while an adult's card may give access to materials from any part of the library. Some libraries believe that it is a parent's right and responsibility to monitor what his or her child is reading, viewing, or using in the library. Others offer the parent the option of restricting his or her child's access to specific parts of the library. Polices on the issuance of library cards and the extent of their use should be developed and adopted by the library board.

The library board policies should state what materials may be borrowed and establish loan periods and overdue fine structures. Because of high demand, the library may shorten loan periods of popular items, such as best-sellers. The loan period may be shortened for items from new or emerging collections, giving more people the opportunity to borrow the items. Some libraries charge a nominal per-day rental fee on certain items, such as videos or DVDs, while other libraries view fees as a form of double taxation and therefore loan all library materials without fees. These are policies that should be discussed and approved by the library board and included in the library's policy manual.

Confidentiality of library records is another important policy area to be considered. Many states have laws regarding the privacy of library records. These laws may prohibit library staff from disclosing who has a library card, what that card has been used to borrow, or who has particular materials. These laws may often prohibit a library from providing a parent with information on the library usage of his or her minor child. State laws may prohibit library staff from sharing any information contained in the customer registration record with anyone who does not have a court order. The 2001 USA Patriot Act even prohibits libraries from disclosing to anyone, other than the library's attorney, when the FBI has issued a court order requesting previously protected registration information. The government has recognized the public's sensitivity to library records and has accorded a high level of privacy to those records; however, the USA Patriot Act does provide governmental access to previously confidential library usage information.

Even though all public libraries loan materials, the way those items are loaned can vary a great deal from library to library. After migrating from a handwritten checkout process or a photographic system, these days most libraries use integrated library system (ILS) computer software to check library materials in and out of the library. ILS vendor software can provide reliable inventory control and remote and in-library access to the library's collection inventory, streamline the day-to-day procedures of staff at the checkout desk, and facilitate the easy sharing of collection information between libraries. Today, even the smallest library can afford to automate the circulation process by using one of the integrated library system vendors, such as *epixtech,* Gaylord Information Systems, Innovative Interfaces, or TLC, or by sharing a system with other area libraries.

In order to take advantage of integrated library systems, a library needs to identify each item in its collection with a unique identifier. This is usually a bar code or radio frequency identification (RFID) tag placed on each item and on every customer library card. The computer will temporarily link borrowed items to individual customer records. When the item is returned, the link is broken. While the item is checked out of the library, its bibliographic record remains in the public access computer, and the date the material is due, but not the borrower's name, is visible on the computer screen. Customers are able to place holds on items checked out and are notified when the item is once again available for loan. The automated system will notify people when the items they have borrowed are overdue and will even generate bills for long overdue items. If people continue to ignore the system messages, the library can electronically turn over the delinquent account to a collection agency or pursue long overdue materials through the local small claims court.

Most libraries are not able to fulfill all of the requests for specific materials at the exact time they are requested. When items owned by the library are checked out to another user, the library will place a hold on the item so that as soon as it returns to the library, the requesting customer is notified of its availability. Many libraries allow the customer to place a hold without staff intervention. Two services, reciprocal borrowing and interlibrary loan, help fill requests for materials not owned by the customer's home library. Reciprocal borrowing allows a customer from one library to use his or her local library card in another library. This is most common when libraries are members of the same library system, network, or consortium. Several states have statewide reciprocal borrowing programs. With the adoption of the National Circulation Interchange Protocol (NCIP), library cards from one library are recognized by the computers from other libraries and allow the customer's record from his or her home library to be temporarily loaded into another library's computer. This makes it more convenient for the borrower and library to facilitate reciprocal borrowing.

Interlibrary loan (ILL) is an agreement between libraries to loan materials to each other so that users of one library can check out materials from another library without having to visit the lending library. The customer orders a specific title at her or his local library, and the library locates and borrows the title on behalf of the customer. The material is delivered to a customer's local library where he or she can check it out and later return it. The local library then returns the material to the lending library. Some libraries charge other libraries modest fees for this service, and the decision to pass the cost on to the customer is made locally by the library board. Libraries not expecting the user to pay for the interlibrary loan might consider the ILL fee as part of their budget for providing materials to all customers.

Interlibrary loan service used to be laborious and time-consuming; technology, however, has increased the ease of ILL. Librarians can now use computers to search multiple library collections at one time and easily locate needed materials.

REFERENCE SERVICE

Cirulation is not the only service that is automated. With the advent of the Internet, traditional reference service has undergone a tremendous change. Historically, books were the main resource used to answer reference questions. Today, librarians use books, magazines, the telephone, and the Internet to answer reference questions. However, though the work methods and resources have changed, the basic concept of reference service for children and adults has stayed the same. In 1955, Samuel Rothstein, former director of the School of Librarianship, University of British Columbia, described reference service as (1) guidance in the use of the library; (2) suggestions for selection of materials; and (3) purveyance of information.[1] Today, reference librarians essentially perform the same three tasks. Reference librarians provide guidance in the use of the library when they teach customers to find, retrieve, analyze, and use information. The resources available for reference and research have expanded far beyond print materials, but reference librarians still use the same skills to retrieve information. Second, reference librarians suggest appropriate resources in the format that the customer needs. Today, this service is called readers' advisory. And third, reference librarians provide answers to specific information requests from library customers. What has changed is the way librarians locate and deliver information. Printed books are still used in daily reference work, but electronic resources, such as computerized indexes and Internet resources, have expanded reference service. These electronic resources allow people to locate information that is too recent to be included in printed books whose publication may take several months. Librarians can now deliver the answers to customer questions in person or by phone, fax, e-mail and, in some libraries, cable television. Some libraries are providing online reference assistance twenty-four hours a day, seven days a week using chat sessions on the Internet or commercially by contracting with companies that provide the service. The changes seen in reference services over the years have been effected more through the delivery mechanisms than in the core service provided.

Good reference service is very dependent on good reference librarians. Joseph Wheeler, former director of the Enoch Pratt Free Library (Baltimore, Md.), listed seven qualities desirable for every reference librarian:

1. Literacy, or the ability to comprehend easily and to receive communication
2. Imagination and resourcefulness
3. Enthusiasm

4. Persistence
5. A sense of media, which makes the good reference librarian a true "master of materials"
6. Humility, so that one doesn't consider it a personal affront if the information cannot be found in the library's collection (and is indefatigable in trying to locate it somewhere else)
7. "Love for serving people, or that spirit of service which we hope motivates all librarians."[2]

Whether serving children or adults, every reference librarian should have these characteristics.

Loaning library materials and providing reference service are done in every public library. As libraries grow, so does the need to provide more specialization, and, in response to this need, libraries begin to create departments within the organization. Usually the departments are age-based; however, some larger libraries may divide into departments based on subject matter. Either way, age or subject, the purpose of departmentalization is to enhance public access to the collection and services.

CHILDREN'S SERVICES

The 1890s saw the opening of children's rooms in large libraries across the nation. By the time of the great burst of branch-library building at the turn of the twentieth century (stimulated by the gifts of Andrew Carnegie), space devoted to children was recognized as a necessity.[3] The spaces for children closely resembled the spaces for adults, but contained materials appropriate for younger readers. The main purpose of library service to children in the early days was to expose children to good literature.

Children's librarians are still interested in providing the best literature to children, but the focus is less didactic. Children are encouraged to read for recreation and entertainment as much as for formal education. Programming for children has become an important tool for attracting children to the library, exposing them to the world of reading, while providing information and building literacy skills.

In 2000, the Public Library Association's Early Literacy Initiative began a partnership with the National Institute of Child Health and Human Development (NICHD), a division of the National Institutes of Health. The study showed that there is nearly a 90 percent probability that a child will remain a poor reader at the end of the fourth grade if the child is a poor reader at the end of the first grade. The study also noted that knowledge of alphabet letters at entry into kindergarten is a strong predictor of reading ability in tenth grade. The strong correlation between the two factors suggests that improving preschoolers' reading readiness is crucial, and public libraries are the ideal setting for this training. Not only are there programs geared to the preschool child, but there are also programs available for the child's adult caregiver. Librarians stress the importance of caregivers talking and reading to young children. The librarian in a story time can serve as a role model for an adult reading to a child—a practice a parent or guardian can continue with the child at home. The preschool materials collection in a public library provides resources—such as ergonomically correct and appropriately sized computer workstations with kid-sized keyboards that are more accommodating to small hands, board books, puppets, book and cassette kits, and picture books—that a parent can use with his or her child at home.

Many public libraries offer programs to babies and toddlers. The purpose of programming for infants and toddlers is to provide language and literature models appropriate for those ages. These models can also provide movement and music, both of which will help the child developmentally in learning language.

Initially, librarians were strictly focused on introducing older children to high-quality literature, but today's children's librarian is also busy helping children find resources for homework assignments, providing readers' advisory service for recreational reading, and providing programming related to children's literature. The children's collection will contain award-winning books and popular reading titles like those included in the Lemony Snicket series. Nonfiction material is readily available to help children complete school assignments or to support scouting badge activities. Books for inquisitive minds on sensitive topics, such as divorce, personal safety, physical development, and sexual orientation, are also available, and librarians can suggest appropriate materials to children.

Creative programming for slightly older children is common in public libraries. With musical performances, book battles, summer reading clubs, and craft activities, there is a wide choice of programs to attract, entertain, and educate children in the public library setting.

Libraries have become such active and attractive places that children unattended by adults often come to the library after school. The public library is seen as a safe haven for children, but it is a public building, and as such, its employees cannot be responsible for unattended children. Many libraries adopt policies stating that staff members cannot assume responsibility for unattended children, especially children who are not picked up before the library closes. During open hours, unattended children may act in a manner not in compliance with the library's code of conduct, and this diverts staff from providing service to other customers. In response to this need, some libraries have created special programs aimed specifically at these "latchkey" children. Library procedures related to unattended children vary a great deal from community to community depending on staffing levels and the number of unattended children coming to the library.

YOUNG ADULT (YA) SERVICES

Specialized service to young adults can be traced to before World War I, but the opening of the country's first teen room, the Robert Louis Stevenson Room at the Cleveland (Ohio) Public Library in 1925, was a landmark. Such facilities spread rapidly after World War II.[4] With people between the ages of thirteen and nineteen accounting for about 13 percent of the U.S. population in 2002, this group continues to need public library services. Teenagers' use of a public library accounts for a large portion of overall library usage; therefore, today's public libraries are focusing more than ever on the library needs of young adults. Teen Central at the Phoenix (Ariz.) Public Library created a teen advisory group to help create a space that attracts and serves teens. By providing resources, both print and electronic, for homework and offering music, games, and information on YA issues, the library has created a very popular resource for teenagers in Phoenix.

Just as teens struggle with the adjustment of moving from childhood to adulthood, librarians have struggled to design appropriate services for this age group. Some libraries serve teens as an adjunct service of the children's room, but teens do not want to be perceived as children. The adult collection may have many of the resources that teens need, but the atmosphere in the adult services area of the library may be less appealing to teens.

There are four criteria for successful service to young adults in the public library: space, staff, resources, and programs. First, there should be a welcoming *space* that is not childish or stuffy, but designed with the tastes of young adults in mind. Young adults have a strong desire to socialize. Library staff should expect activity in the room to be noisier than that typically heard in an adult services area. By creating a special YA room, the public library can provide the best service possible without compromising library use by other age groups. Furniture should be movable, comfortable, and more casual than that in other parts of the library.

Second, *staff members* designated to work with young adults need to be understanding and sympathetic to teens, while at the same time setting behavior parameters that will allow teens to be comfortable in the library without infringing on the comfort of other people using the library. Staff members need to maintain relationships not only with the teens coming to the library, but also with other professionals, such as schoolteachers, who work with young adults so coordination of programs and services is achieved.

The third criterion of successful teen service is the *resources* provided in the young adult area. The lifeblood of any teen department is normally the fiction collection, particularly in paperback; however, many studies say magazines are teens' most popular print material. Teens use nonfiction from other parts of the library, but most teens looking for recreational or assigned fiction reading find themselves in the YA area.[5] Also of particular interest to teens are nonprint or interactive materials. Music defines and reflects each generation: Identifying and including the type of CDs, DVDs, and videos that meet the interests of young adults is essential to the success of this service.

Just as paperbacks are preferred over hardbound books, teens often prefer accessing materials in electronic format. Computers are an integral part of teenagers' lives and need to be included in YA spaces. Whether they are used to access the Internet or to play games, computers should be in ample supply in the YA area.

The fourth criterion of successful public library service to young adults is *programs and services*. Just as the children's room library staff provides programs that are age appropriate, YA staff should plan programs that will appeal to young adults. Programs on creative writing or crafts, or presentations on such topics as urban legends or how to get a summer job as well as more traditional library programs, such as summer reading clubs, have proven popular with young adults. However, the best public library program may be doomed to failure if it conflicts with school schedules or special activities and events at local middle and high schools.

Creating a young adult advisory council is an excellent way to gather input from young adults on library space planning, programs, and services that appeal to them. The advisory council also is a social opportunity for young adults as well as a future support group for the library.

Many children develop a love of reading at an early age. If these young readers are to become lifelong library users, it is essential that their participation in and use of the public library continue through the busy and tumultuous teen years. A well-designed young adult service will go a long way toward attracting this age group and keeping them interested in the library.

ADULT SERVICES

Lifelong learning is critical in today's changing society. Whether exploring new career opportunities, planning vacations, doing home repair, or researching personal investments, adults will continue to need information throughout their lives. Adults often turn to the public library as their information source. In 1998, the Gallup Organization conducted a survey for the American Library Association and found 66 percent of Americans had used a public library at least once during the last year either in person, by telephone, or online. Sixty-five percent had consulted a librarian.[6] Despite superbookstores, video stores, health clubs, and home computers vying for the attention of adults, Americans continue to use their public libraries in record numbers.

Adults use the local public library for lifelong learning in such areas as cooking, home decorating, crafts, auto repair, and gardening. Adults use the library's business resources for career exploration and job searches, resume writing, and personal investment research. They borrow materials on a wide variety of self-help issues and parenting.

Those who are enrolled in a formal education program from high school through graduate school often return to their local public libraries for supplemental reading materials. Study guides for the General Education Degree (GED), the SAT I and II, the Graduate Record Examination (GRE), or other professional school admission tests and even civil service exams are readily available at most public libraries.

Adult services librarians also provide readers' advisory services in both fiction and nonfiction areas. By using readers' advisory tools or personal experience, librarians can help people find the latest best-seller, the next book in a series, or just a good book to read.

As mentioned earlier, libraries today are far more than books, and one of the most popular resources provided by public libraries is Internet access. With over 95 percent of American public libraries having Internet connections, almost everyone can access the Internet.[7] In addition to making the connection available, libraries purchase books and offer programs on how to navigate and evaluate web resources. But library customers do not have to do all the searching on their own. Librarians direct researchers to reliable and pertinent websites. In some libraries, this service is provided around the clock, if not by a librarian then at least through the library's website.

Programming for adults is also a part of public library service. In many cases, speakers present library programs on such topics as estate planning, investments, or travel. Smaller group programs, such as book discussions or computer training, provide a hands-on approach to programming. The topics included in public library programs for adults will vary widely depending on other resources and interests of the community.

SPECIAL SERVICES

People with disabilities or older adults experiencing limited mobility or lower vision may find the library difficult to use. To respond to these needs, libraries have developed special services, collections, and programs. Libraries provide special services not just because it is the law (Americans with Disabilities Act, 1990), but also because it is the right thing to do. A library does not have to invest large amounts of money to serve people with disabilities. Resources at reasonable prices, such as large-print books, audio books, and captioned DVDs and videos, can be routinely purchased with funds from the library's regular materials budget.

Libraries with more financial resources available may want to include assistive technology. *Assistive technology* is the term used to describe equipment designed to help an individual develop, maintain, or improve his or her ability to function daily. In a library these technologies could range from small, inexpensive low-vision aids like magnifying lenses to closed-circuit TVs that enlarge print, personalized readers, TDDs (telecommunications devices for the deaf), a motorized wheelchair for use in the library, and computers controlled by voice or voice software that makes print materials audible.

Even if a library has a separate area, the latest assistive technology, and excellent funding, the attitude of the staff and administrators is the most important factor in outreach services. Staff training videos, like *People First,* provide excellent guidance on working with people with disabilities.[8] Conferences like the annual Closing the Gap conference held each fall in Minnesota provide information on special techniques and equipment to improve service to the disabled student.

The staff must be willing to go the extra step in providing customized services to people with very special needs. In addition to creativity and patience, the staff will need fortitude, because this service, like no other library service, often does not have a happy ending. Customers may move out of independent living situations to assisted living care or nursing homes that are out of the library's service area. Elderly or infirm customers will die. And, while providing very personalized service can be rewarding to librarians, the eventual loss of a customer hurts more because the service has been so personalized.

Some libraries have separate mission statements for their outreach services. The mission of the Rochester Hills (Mich.) Public Library's Outreach Services Department is to identify individuals with special needs (including elderly, sight or hearing impaired, or functionally illiterate) and to assist them in gaining access to needed library services.[9] The Outreach Services Department also creates new programs and services to attract new library users. The Rochester Hills program is a multifaceted approach to enable individuals with special needs to maintain independence and enhance personal growth. By providing easy access to library resources and specialized services and by offering challenging enrichment programs, the library hopes to increase options in the areas of education, leisure time activities, and information access.

Low-vision service is one of the most common specialized services offered in public libraries. Although the choice of large-print titles is not as large as that of regular print titles, many popular fiction and nonfiction titles are published in large print at the same time as is the regular print edition. Low-vision service can include things as simple as book pillows and low-vision reading aids, such as nonprescription magnifying lenses that will enlarge print up to ten times. More elaborate equipment may also be considered, including such items as a handheld closed-circuit television system that magnifies up to sixty times and allows persons with low vision to view such materials as photographs, coins, stamps, and handwritten notes, or scanning and reading equipment that will convert printed text to an audio product. Computers equipped with speech software also can make web resources available to the visually impaired. This equipment costs between $5 and $5,000, and many units can be loaned for home use.

Some services may be locally based while others, like the services to the blind and physically handicapped supported by the Library of Congress, are available through any public library in the United States. Outreach service also has no age limit. Whether the homebound or disabled person is a child or an older adult, the library should be able to tailor services and provide resources to meet each person's library and information needs.

People living with hearing impairments can also be served by the public library. Assistive technology that allows the hearing impaired to participate in discussions, whether one-on-one or in large groups, is available. These personal listening systems can be kept at the service desk for use by staff providing service to people in the library, used at library-sponsored programs, or loaned to interested individuals.

TDDs are available using software and a modem that is connected to a staff member's computer. Messages typed and sent to the library by people with hearing impairments will be displayed on the screen, notifying the staff that a hearing-impaired person needs assistance. Separate TDDs are also available, but unless they are located in a highly trafficked or visible area, library staff is apt to miss the messages. Assistance can also be given using low-tech methods, such as paper and pencils for writing notes to communicate with library staff.

For people with limited mobility yet able to visit the library, the availability of a motorized wheelchair, as seen in many retail outlets, will make physical movement around the library easier. Drive-up window service for materials return and pickup saves people from getting out of their cars to enter the building. Automatic doors and power-assist doors into the library and all rest rooms make the building more convenient for those with mobility challenges.

Challenges to library use are not limited to individuals with physical disabilities. Many people are not able to get to the library because they are in institutions. The economically disfranchised, the illiterate, the emotionally or learning disabled, and individuals who are incarcerated are also entitled to public library service. Some libraries overcome this inaccessibility by providing bookmobile service to nursing homes, day-care facilities, or senior centers. Other libraries establish deposit collections in social service agencies and prisons. Each library needs to evaluate the specific needs of its community and the resources already provided by other agencies before designing outreach services. What will be good service in one community might not be appropriate in another, but all communities will have people who need special outreach service from the public library.

CONCLUSION

Although all public libraries loan library materials and provide reference service, there are many other services that can be offered. Based on its existing community resources, the demographic makeup of the community, or geographic barriers in each location, the library will plan and develop appropriate services for its specific community.

Public libraries should offer something for everyone. Programs and resources for preschoolers and children in elementary school need to be marketed to the parents and caregivers who bring the children to the library. Children involved and familiar with the library continue to use the library through their teen years if appropriate space, programs, and resources are provided. Out-of-school adults will use the library for recreational reading, vocational information, and support of lifelong learning, and people with special needs can find information and recreation at their public library.

Whether focusing on children, teens, adults, older adults, or people with disabilities, the library can become a second home to everyone in the community. It is the place where people go for information, recreation, and a smile that says, "Welcome to your public library."

NOTES

1. Samuel Rothstein, *The Development of Reference Services through Academic Traditions, Public Library Practice and Special Librarianship* (Chicago: Association of College and Research Libraries, 1955), 102.
2. Joseph Wheeler, *Practical Administration of Public Libraries* (New York: Harper and Row, 1981), 177.
3. Whitney North Seymour and Elizabeth N. Layne, *For the People: Fighting for Public Libraries* (Garden City, N.Y.: Doubleday, 1979), 23.
4. Wheeler, *Practical Administration of Public Libraries*, 203.
5. Patrick Jones, *Connecting Young Adults and Libraries* (New York: Neal-Schuman, 1999), 114.
6. ALA Library Fact Sheet, Public Library Use, 2002. Available at www.ala.org/library/fact6.html. Accessed 17 November 2002.
7. John Carlo Bertot and Charles R. McClure, *Public Libraries and the Internet 2000* (Washington, D.C.: NCLIS, 2000 Web Release Version), 3.
8. *People First* (Chicago: ALA, 1990).
9. Outreach Mission Statement, 2002. Available at www.rhpl.org/OutreachMission Statement.html. Accessed 17 November 2002.

13

Promoting the Library

At first blush one might think that public libraries have no competitors. After all, each town only has one public library.

In fact, public libraries have many competitors, particularly from the for-profit market.

If libraries are to remain viable, they must promote and market new and traditional library services and not rely upon the perception that libraries are a public good. Librarians must deliver the right information to the right person at the right time in the right format and make people believe that libraries are the best and first source of information.

Our consumer-oriented society creates competition between libraries and retail bookstores, online bookstores, Internet service providers, web-based tools, publish-on-demand services, video stores, and entertainment venues. In some instances, for-profit businesses mimic and compete with traditional library services by providing such programs as story times and author talks. In other instances, the retail community offers services for a fee, such as home delivery and personalized shopping, that are not typically available at public libraries.

To remain competitive, businesses and libraries need to use their human and technological resources effectively. Public libraries need to focus on the unique services they can provide, such as free loan service, personalized reference service, and reliable referrals to resources. Libraries need to know when to use technology to work smarter and when to rely on the human intervention of library staff when special assistance is desired or needed.

A cost-effective tool that was once thought to threaten the existence of the public library is the Internet; however, a recent Urban Libraries Council

(ULC) study showed that 75.2 percent of Internet users also used the library, 60.3 percent of library users also used the Internet, and 40 percent of the survey population used both.[1]

In some communities, the public library may be the only point of Internet access available free to residents. Free Internet access brings people to their local library. Instead of competing with the public library, the Internet actually introduces some people to the public library. This is due in part to the way libraries offer and market Internet service. Libraries offer faster broadband connections that deliver web pages faster than many home Internet services. Libraries provide the computers that many people cannot afford in their homes. Once such users are in the library, the librarians can introduce them to traditional library services as well as to enhanced Internet services.

Equipment and connections are just part of the reason library Internet service is popular. The most important enhancement is the librarian's contribution to Internet usage. Librarians use traditional library skills, such as the indexing and organization of information, to create user-friendly and reliable websites that meet community interests and needs. The librarian becomes the human search engine that finds and delivers Internet resources to library users.

TELLING THE STORY

Libraries offer valuable programs and services, but simply offering programs and services does not mean that the public will use them. Increased library use comes through awareness, and awareness comes through promotion. The library must promote its services by

- positioning library board and staff members in other community organizations,
- preparing articles for library or municipal publications,
- preparing articles for local newspapers,
- creating flyers and posters, and, if possible,
- producing public service announcements for local television or radio broadcasts.

Positioning key library board and staff members in community service organizations and on the boards of other nonprofit organizations is a great way to make people aware of and supportive of the library. Staff members who live or are active in the community can deliver the library's message on a one-on-one basis to friends, neighbors, and other community leaders. Not only can staff active in these groups or organizations personally deliver the library's message, the library is positioned to receive public support, gifts, and recognition from the same organizations. Having a seat at the table with community movers and shakers is valuable for the library. Although delivering the library's message in a one-on-one environment is effective, it is limited in its range. The library can deliver the same message in written formats, such as press releases, newsletters, or flyers. Many municipal governments regularly send out newsletters to every home and business letting people know what is going on in the municipality. This is an ideal way to keep the community informed about the municipality and can be used by a library to promote its programs and services. *Municipal newsletters* are particularly appealing because the library usually does not have to pay for the production and mailing of the newsletter. Whether it is a brief 500-word article in the municipal newsletter or a multipage library newsletter, newsletters offer the library the opportunity to tell its story in its own words. The advantage is that the newsletter goes to everyone and is free. The disadvantage is that some people view newsletters as junk mail. The library must strive to make its printed message attractive enough to catch the reader's eye.

Local newspapers are another way to distribute library information. People subscribe to newspapers and are more likely to read them than municipal or library newsletters. Most community newspapers welcome press releases announcing library programs or services and will print those releases as a service to the public. At the same time, press releases offer libraries the opportunity to provide information on special events, new services, and programs. Not every press release needs to highlight a new service. Many people are not aware of basic public library services, such as telephone reference, interlibrary loan, or even story times, so press releases can highlight many standard library services that the public may not know of or remember. The advantage of press releases is that the library can generate them; the disadvantage is that newspapers cannot run every press release received and may not have space available for time-dated library news.

Promoting the library either in person or in print outside of the library is another way to reach new customers, but libraries should not ignore in-library promotion. Salespeople know that it is much harder to get a new customer than it is to keep the one they already have. *Posters, flyers, and bookmarks* promoting library events should be available in the library for pickup by current library customers. Even people who use the library on a daily or weekly basis are generally only aware of a small portion of the library's services. The young mother or father bringing a small child to story time may not be aware that the library offers telephone reference. The college student using the library's collection for research may not be aware that library resources can help him or her prepare a resume or conduct a job search. Readers of popular materials may not know they can place holds on materials that are checked out or that they can place purchase requests with library staff for materials the library does not already own. Through posters, flyers, and bookmarks, libraries can inform people who are regularly using the library about services that might be of interest to them. The advantage of in-library promotion is that the audience is already predisposed to use the library. There are no disadvantages to in-library promotions as long as internal promotion is not the only promotion being done by the library.

Using *public service announcements* (PSAs) may be a viable option to some libraries. Television and radio broadcasters must air public service announcements to fulfill their FCC licensing requirements. Some stations may even be willing to produce a ten-, thirty-, or sixty-second public service announcement for the library, while others will accept library-provided PSAs in written form. Libraries may have the resources to prepare their own PSAs or may purchase generic announcements from the American Library Association or library suppliers. Regardless of the source, it is essential that the announcements be of the highest broadcast quality because commercial radio and television stations will not air amateurish material. The advantage of PSAs is that they can reach audiences that are not familiar with, or regular users of, the library. The disadvantages are that they can be difficult and expensive to produce and the library will have no say as to when they are broadcast.

SPECIAL EVENTS

Libraries have many opportunities to host special events that can celebrate onetime occasions, such as groundbreakings, grand openings, and dedications of exhibits, or that can be repeated events, such as fund-raisers. Successful special events take a great deal of time to plan and execute; however, these events can raise the library's visibility in the community, raise money for library services and programs, or both. There must be an obvious reason to sponsor such events, one that is important enough to justify the amount of time and effort that will be required.

The key to successful events is to allow sufficient planning time. Depending on the size of the event, planning should begin from four to twelve months before the event. Before a planning committee is formed, the library must identify the purpose or goal of the event. Will it be a friend-raiser or a fund-raiser? Where and when should the event be held? How large a budget will be needed to plan and execute the event?

Once these very basic decisions are made, a planning committee can be established. Planning committees composed of people having a variety of talents and perspectives will help make the event successful. The committee will need people with high visibility in the community, people with good planning and marketing skills, and people who are willing to do the actual hands-on work. The committee should have representatives from the library board, staff, volunteers, and other people who use and support the library. People involved in the planning will form a stronger bond with the library and a commitment to the event and to the library. Special events are terrific opportunities to connect high-profile community leaders to the library and to position the library as the organization that community leaders support.

Whether a community celebration or library fund-raiser, special events offer opportunities to showcase the library, honor library supporters, or raise money for the library. Pre- and post-event coverage should include press releases announcing the formation of the planning committee, the purpose and date of the event, and the results of the event and a thank-you to all who helped or attended. Each press release will keep the public informed of the event and will make them more aware of the library.

Although the special event focuses on one activity, it can be a means to create more community awareness of the library. It can create new collaborations between the library and other organizations. It is an opportunity to showcase the library in the community.

SIGNAGE, EXHIBITS, AND DISPLAYS

Not every public relations event needs to be big and splashy. Public relations can begin at a library's front door with good signage. Having the library's name prominently displayed on the outside of the library where people can see it from a main road reminds people that they have a local library and entices them to come in and use it.

Good signage should also continue throughout the interior. Interior signage will help people find their way around the library. The best directional aid for a library visitor is a helpful staff person; however, good signage will also help library visitors help themselves. A map showing the library layout along with a directory listing specialized services should be easily visible from the library's main entrance. Easy-to-read overhead signage can help people find specific collections or services.

Signs are not a onetime purchase. When a new library opens, a minimum number of signs should be in place; however, after the library has been open for several months, it should reevaluate the number and placement of signs. Sometimes a sign is in the wrong place, or the public does not understand the phrasing or the words on the signs. Additional signs may be needed to help people navigate the library. It may take several months for these needs to surface, so the library should be prepared to make adjustments.

Another effective public relations tool in libraries is the use of exhibits and displays. Display partnerships with community organizations and businesses are another way of introducing nonusers to the library. The local historical society might be interested in displaying local artifacts as part of a library display. The library might work with a local arts organization to sponsor a community art show. If a child's art is on display in the library, that child's parents or grandparents are likely to visit the library to view that art.

Not only can exhibits and displays enhance the library, they can also highlight library services and resources. Special weeks like National Library Week or Banned Books Week offer opportunities to talk about the library's purpose and services. Displays can be set up around holiday themes, such as handmade Christmas gifts, recipes to make the holidays special, or books to help plan a dream vacation. The librarian can do something as simple as pulling books from the collection and putting them on a shelf with a sign saying "Good Reads You Might Have Missed."

Exhibits and displays can be simple or elaborate. They can highlight something in the library or feature something from outside the library. They can be used to attract nonusers to the library or to inform people who are already in the building on issues or topics of interest. Whether the library staff is responsible for scheduling and assembling exhibits and displays or whether a volunteer is in charge, the library should have a written policy outlining acceptable material (see figure 13-1).

CUSTOMER SERVICE

The library staff is the most effective public relations tool the library has. Customers who are made to feel welcome and are treated to top-notch service will want to visit again. Libraries need to work with current customers to make sure they are getting the services they need and want. For this reason it

FIGURE 13-1   Displays and Solicitation Policy

**Displays and Solicitation Policy
of the
Clinton-Macomb (Mich.) Public Library**

As an educational and cultural institution and as part of its public service, the Library welcomes exhibits and displays of interest, information, and enlightenment to the community. The Library provides information to the community through displays, handouts, announcements, and exhibits in designated areas.

1. *Displays*

   A. Priority and Approval: The Library retains priority rights to all exhibit and display space for library purposes. Approval for all exhibits and displays rests with the Library Director or appointed designee(s). Unapproved materials will be disposed of at the Library's discretion.

   B. Eligibility and Space Availability: The Library or other nonprofit organizations, community groups, individuals or governmental agencies may provide materials. Exhibit and display space is available on an equitable basis, regardless of the beliefs or affiliations of individuals or groups requesting this service.

   C. Limitations: The Library reserves the right to limit the size and number of items, the schedule of any display, and the frequency with which the group or organization may have a display.

   D. Endorsement: Distribution or posting of materials by the Library does not necessarily indicate the Library's endorsement of the issue or events promoted by those materials.

   E. Fees: All exhibits and displays are offered to the Library on a voluntary, non-fee basis.

   F. Security and Liability: The Library assumes no liability in the event of damage, destruction, or theft of a display.

   G. Sponsorship Line: A sponsorship line, i.e., a sign stating the sponsorship of the display, may be included; however, values of displayed items will not be included.

2. *Petitioning*

   The Library allows petitioning, distribution of literature or leaflets, canvassing or similar types of appeals by members of the public no closer than five feet either side of the Library's public entrances. This activity must not interfere with building or parking lot ingress or egress.

3. *Sales*

   The Library does not allow panhandling or the sale of goods or services by members of the public in the library building, on the grounds, or in the parking lot. The only merchandising activities permitted are Library or Friends of the Library sponsored sales or activities.

is essential that all library employees are committed to providing the best in customer service.

Libraries need to design and offer breakthrough service. These are services that revolutionize an entire industry's rules of the game by setting new standards for consistently meeting or exceeding customers' service needs and expectations.[2] Most organizations approach service through customer satisfaction. They measure customer satisfaction after the service is provided. However, breakthrough service organizations design services with the customer in mind. They know who that customer is and what she or he needs, and they determine the best way to deliver that service.

This commitment must prevail at all levels of the library organization. The library board and director must provide the time and training the staff needs to provide good service. When a library is understaffed, everyone rushes through his or her work. Library staff should be given enough time to focus on each customer's question or need. A hurried pace is transmitted to the customer and says "We don't have time for you." Having sufficient staff is the first step toward providing noteworthy customer service.

The second element to successful customer service is training. Library staff members need to know how to give good service. Approaching library users with a smile and asking an open-ended question like "How may I help you?" are simple and friendly ways to connect with library customers. A question like "How did you like this book?" indicates that the staff member is thinking about what he or she is doing when checking in returned materials and helps create a dialogue with the library user. Staff members who greet library users by name make them feel welcome in the library.

Scott Cook, chairman of Intuit Software's executive committee, says the real goal of offering great customer service is to create apostles. Intuit Software produced Quicken, a personal and small-business software package that sells for about $50 and has captured more than half the market. Quicken's success is based on extremely high customer satisfaction and loyalty. This is achieved by saturating each stage of product development, design, packaging, and marketing with customer feedback. Customers are invited to participate in the design and packaging processes and in the writing of manuals. The company maintains a customer support phone line. When customers do have questions, they call the support line. People from all layers of the organization—including the CEO—regularly staff these phones. This information is collected, analyzed, and used by design and development staff to create new products, upgrades, and services. Customers are so satisfied with Intuit products that they become "apostles," enabling the company to sell its products with a very small sales force.

Libraries can follow the Intuit model of service. Libraries spend a lot of time and money on attracting new patrons. However, providing good customer service is the key to keeping those patrons. By involving library customers in designing new services and reviewing existing ones, libraries are able to identify their strengths and weaknesses. By matching services and collections to customer needs and reactions, the library can constantly improve. Staff members alert to customer reactions can solve service problems and suggest enhancements. By focusing on customer needs and interests, librarians can design services that will be used and appreciated by the public. Customers who appreciate the services and resources offered by the public library will be more likely to become library apostles.

In 1988, the very small Glendale (Colo.) Public Library noticed an increase in Russian-speaking refugee families. The library staff recognized the need to build collections to serve this growing local population. Russian-speaking staff members were hired. The library became a bilingual branch with translators always available. Programs were created focusing on helping people who spoke English as a second language. By recognizing a community need and involving the community in designing services, this library has grown rapidly and become an essential part of the community.[3]

CONCLUSION

Building a great library and offering great services and resources are not enough to keep a public library vital. If unused and unappreciated, the library will not survive in today's competitive society. Public librarians have to be proactive about the work they do and make sure that the community knows what is available at and through its public library.

The library story has to be communicated both inside and outside the library, and the mark of a successful library public relations program is that library users promote the library to their friends, family, and neighbors. Making library users apostles is not easy. It takes a strong commitment on the part of library administration, staff, and users to broadcast the library's message of service and information provision. A concerted public relations program can go a long way toward making the library the center of the community, able to take on any competition that may come along.

NOTES

1. Internet Study Fact Sheet (home page of the Urban Libraries Council, 2002). Available at www.urbanlibraries.org/Internet%20Study%20Fact%20Sheet.html. Accessed 17 November 2002.
2. James L. Heskett, W. Earl Sasser, and Christopher W. L. Hart, *Service Breakthroughs: Changing the Rules of the Game* (New York: Free Press, 1990), iii.
3. Kathleen de la Peña McCook, *A Place at the Table* (Chicago: ALA, 2002), 56–59.

Index